What People Are Saying About
The Politically Incorrect Jesus

"A thoughtful and insightful look into how to be true to God and yourself."

DELILAH
National Radio Host

"No one who reads *The Politically Incorrect Jesus* will ever view cultural PC the same way again. In bold, no-nonsense, biblically based expressions, Joe Battaglia strips the facade off the culture war and warns believers against the dangers of being seduced by it. The book is a game changer."

LARRY W. POLAND, PH.D.
Chairman, Mastermedia International

"In an era when the Church seems to either be so politically correct that its message is ineffective, or so abrasive that it offends without enlightening anyone, my friend Joe Battaglia calls us to see that Jesus came to redeem the culture and not to condemn it. Jesus' Church is designed to bring real hope and joy to a superficial culture by living out the truth in a way that meets people at their point of deepest need. Joe shows us that being countercultural does not mean being against people, but for peace and love. If you're tired of the culture wars, this book is a must-read for you."

JIM LISKE
President and CEO, Prison Fellowship Ministries

"My friend Joe Battaglia exposes the ease with which many rewrite the teachings of Jesus. Jesus said of H' *truth, and the life; no one comes to the* sounds anything but inclusive. Batta; society and individuals to return to th

Christ, a truth entered through relationship, and the only truth that still sets us free."

DAVID JONES
Vice President, The Palau Association

"This is an important book. It's a wake-up call to a slumbering Church and culture, a reminder of what is true not what is popular. I highly recommend it."

SHEILA WALSH
Author of *The Storm Inside*

"In *The Politically Incorrect Jesus*, my friend Joe Battaglia presents an intelligent and common sense approach to how a person of faith can stand up to the current issues in culture that would divide us without pointing fingers or engaging in the culture war. He has interesting perspectives that we would all do well to consider on how to be followers of Jesus to a world that wants to see the real thing."

MICHAEL W. SMITH
Singer/Songwriter

"Joe Battaglia says what needs to be said about the dangers and impact of our politically correct world. It's a needed wake-up call to our culture! This is a MUST READ for anyone wanting to understand our times."

ALEX KENDRICK
Filmmaker, *Facing the Giants, Fireproof, Courageous*

"I've just finished reading *The Politically Incorrect Jesus* and I'm angry. In fact, there is enough in this book to tick off almost everybody. But the great thing about the book is that what starts in anger, moves to conviction, then to repentance and ultimately to action. We've drifted so far and most of us don't know a way back. This book is a road map for getting back. I've decided to no longer 'shillyshally.' You will too!"

DR. STEVE BROWN
Author/President, Key Life Radio Network

"With candor and courage, Joe Battaglia takes on some of the madness of our day as attention is focused beyond the noise of political correctness to the person of Jesus. Timeless truths drawn from HIS life and love are presented with clarity and grace as firm foundations for purposeful and strategic living in our contemporary world. Read it and REAP!"

DAVID FERGUSON
Co-chairman, Awakening America Alliance

"Unfortunately, we live in a world where black and white have become dingy gray, and God's call to be salt and light has been met by dim and tasteless Christians. Joe sounds a clarion call to be men and women of holiness and distinction, those who shine like stars in the midst of a crooked and twisted world (Philippians 2:15). Where political correctness collides with biblical truth, this book will challenge you to hold fast to the unchanging principles and promises of God's Word."

MICHAEL CATT
Senior Pastor, Sherwood Baptist Church, Albany, Georgia

"Thank you, Joe, for writing *The Politically Incorrect Jesus*. I learned so much. I now completely understand my ethnicity, my color, my race. I'm a 'Christ-follower.' That's it. I've been born again for thirty years and so blessed because of that simple decision a long time ago. After so much time passing, I just feel that your book is the definitive statement in tying my faith in Jesus all together for me."

TOM GEHRING
Lawyer and author of *Settle It! . . . and be Blessed*

"My dear friend Joe Battaglia makes a cogent and powerful case for how we have allowed our culture and politically correct thought to shape our thinking and lives, regardless of whether we believe those things to be true. This book is a gentle, yet forceful reminder, of standing up for what one believes. I highly recommend it."

RITA COSBY
Emmy-winning TV host and best-selling author

"My friend Joe Battaglia understands that Christians make a difference in this world by being different from this world. They don't make a difference by being the same. Unlike the world around them, Christians are called to be theologians of mercy rather than philosophers of might. Whether they realize it or not, the world desperately needs to hear our confession more than they need to see our competence. They need to hear that we are weak and needy and desperate. And the good news is that Christians are free to admit this without fear because our worth and value and significance are not dependent on our strength, what we do, or what others think. Our identity is firmly anchored in what Jesus has done for us. Thank you for this reminder, Joe. I keep forgetting."

TULLIAN TCHIVIDJIAN
Founder of Liberate and author of
One Way Love: Inexhaustible Grace for an Exhausted World

"Jesus is dangerous. And so is this wonderful book, because Joe shows us a Jesus who simply refuses to give us what we want: Affirmation of our own biases. Instead, He challenges us to change, to love, and to simply embrace the truth about ourselves, no matter how unfashionable. This is a book we need. Now."

BRANT HANSEN
Radio host and author of
Unoffendable: How Just One Change Can Make All of Life Better

THE
Politically
Incorrect
Jesus

Living BOLDLY in
a CULTURE of UNBELIEF

JOE BATTAGLIA

BroadStreet
PUBLISHING

The Politically Incorrect Jesus
© 2014 by Joseph Battaglia

ISBN: 978-1-4245-4981-8 (paperback)
ISBN: 978-1-4245-5008-1 (e-book)

Published by BroadStreet Publishing Group, LLC
Racine, Wisconsin, USA
www.broadstreetpublishing.com

All Scripture is taken from THE HOLY BIBLE, NEW INTERNATIONAL VERSION®. NIV®. Copyright © 1973, 1978, 1984 by International Bible Society. Used by permission of Zondervan. All rights reserved.

Cover design by Garborg Design Works, Inc. at www.garborgdesign.com
Interior typesetting by Katherine Lloyd, www.TheDESKonline.com
Edited by Ramona Cramer Tucker

Stock or custom editions of BroadStreet Publishing titles may be purchased in bulk for educational, business, ministry, fundraising, or sales promotional use. For information, please e-mail info@broadstreetpublishing.com.

Printed in the United States of America.

15 16 17 18 19 20   7 6 5 4 3 2 1

To my family…both those who have made me
who I am and have passed on and those who
continue to impact me daily by their love and presence in
my life. Especially my wife, LuAnn, and daughter, Alanna,
who are testaments of God's presence
and favor in my life.

Contents

Foreword by Eric Metaxas

I'm so thrilled my dear friend Joe Battaglia has written this book! As those of us who know Joe would expect, it's chock full of wisdom. Joe just happens to have the gift of making wisdom sound matter-of-fact, and when he says something profound, you almost have the feeling that you came up with it yourself!

Just thinking about this reminds me of when I met Joe, back in the fall of 1999. My daughter was three months old, and my wife and I had just decided we were moving to the Big City! So we loaded up our old rusted Ford pickup and hauled our belongings clean across this great country of ours. It was quite a journey, and then some! Snow drifts taller'n ye ever seen! Mountain lions a-leapin' in front of the truck! And a herd o' bison stretchin' clean to the horizon and back—*twice!*

I'm terribly sorry. I've had a chronic cough and I'm not getting any sleep, so my brain is a little foggy. Now that I think of it, we never owned any rusted Ford pickup! I have no idea why I said that. As I recall, we drove a rented U-Haul. And we certainly didn't drive across the country! We just drove about an hour south on the Merritt Parkway from Connecticut! But we really did move to Manhattan. That much I know for sure.

The reason I met Joe was that I had just gotten a job working as a writer for VeggieTales! During that time I got to write a Hamlet/Omelet parody for their *Lyle the Kindly Viking* video. And I even got to be the voice of the narrator on their *Esther* video! Yes, I got to be the voice in a cartoon! Unfortunately the narrator is off camera, so I don't know for sure what vegetable I was supposed to be playing. If I had to guess, I'd say broccoli rabe.

In any case, as a result of my brand new job with VeggieTales, I was officially working "in the media," so I got an invitation to join an exclusive by-invitation-only "Men's Media Bible Study" that met right in the Empire State Building! All the guys in the Bible study worked in the media. At least they had at some point. Unfortunately, quite a few of them were unemployed. But the upside was that they had plenty of time to go to Bible studies! And one of the employed guys in the group was Joe Battaglia.

Um, the warden just told me I had five more minutes, so I think I'd better stop goofing around and get to the point. I remember during those Bible studies in the Empire State Building, Joe would get talking about a passage of Scripture and you'd think to yourself, "Holy cow! This guy really knows his stuff. Where'd he come from?" Of course, everybody knew Joe came in from Jersey; he drove or took the PATH train. But that's not what I meant. What I meant was he really knew the Bible and he really knew what it meant and he could always help us understand what it meant for each of us in our lives at that time! That's wisdom, friends! And it's in mighty short supply nowadays. So this book is just what the doctor ordered.

So for all of you who had jobs and couldn't attend that wonderful Bible study in the Empire State Building, you're in for a real treat. Okay, warden, I'm ready.

Eric Metaxas
Author, speaker, TV host

Introduction

Want to provoke controversy and a variety of intense emotions? Just mention the name "Jesus." Throughout history, he's been admired and ridiculed, revered and rejected, dismissed and embraced. In today's increasingly secular society, where diversity, tolerance, and other politically correct concepts are prized, many seek to de-deify Him so He can fit into a politically correct context in which all "truth" is equal and there is a more open-minded approach to "spirituality."

But Jesus was not open-minded when it came to truth. He stated that He was THE truth, which flies in the face of political correctness. Much of what He taught and stood for clearly clashes with the popular notions that want to redefine and reinterpret the person and teachings of Jesus, and ultimately the Christian faith, so that neither step on anyone's sensitivities.

What is "political correctness"? For the purposes of this book, I define it as:

The "chic" moral ideology of the day advocated and fleshed out in the public square by self-appointed gatekeepers of public opinion to the point where that definition becomes "fashionable."

But who exactly are these self-appointed gatekeepers, and what is their agenda? Are they, perhaps, trying to replace the Christian faith with a moral ideology all their own? One in which no one can state the obvious, for fear that exposing truth would be disturbing to someone? Ultimately, political correctness boldly asks us to commit intellectual suicide by assenting to what we actually do not believe. It asks us to buy into the fashionable definition of Jesus to make Him and His teachings more palatable, in an expedient way to "relate" to a wider world.

Jesus, however, calls us to be salt and light, not chameleons. If we are Christ's representatives on earth, changing colors may allow us to blend in, but it will be at the expense of our integrity and Jesus' admonition for us to follow His words, which are life.

Jesus calls us to be salt
and light, not chameleons.

We live in a time where the issues of the day are overwhelming. We are over-stimulated, due to the constant flow of media through our minds, and so overstressed and tired that, on some days, we can't even decide which pair of socks to wear in the morning. We need to grasp hold of a faith that can meet us right in the trenches of life and help us see past what is all around us. A faith that is THE center of our lives, with everything revolving around that. The kind of faith that acts as a filter for everything we experience everyday—in media, entertainment, politics, relationships, and yes, even in the church.

It is my prayer that *The Politically Incorrect Jesus* will enlighten others regarding the issues and ideology in our current cultural climate, as juxtaposed with the clear teachings of Jesus, and urge readers to embrace being who God Almighty designed them to be: men and women of counterculture faith, making a difference in a counterfeit world.

Then Jesus cried out, "When a man believes in me, he does not believe in me only, but in the one who sent me. When he looks at me, he sees the one who sent me. I have come into the world as a light, so that no one who believes in me should stay in darkness."

—JOHN 12:44–46

When we raise the flag higher
than the cross,
we have a problem.

1

The Culture War

When I was a kid, the Cold War was at its height. It was the United States against the Soviet Union. We exported democracy, and the USSR exported communism. East against the West. They wore the black hats. We wore the white ones. It was easy to tell who the enemy was. Our cartoons even exploited it. Boris and Natasha against Rocky and Bullwinkle.

It was called "the Cold War" because of the frozen stalemate between the two superpowers. No one was really fighting each other. It was one big standoff, fraught with innuendo, threats of nuclear war, bluster, and bluffing. Americans were united against this common threat.

Fast forward a generation. After the Berlin Wall fell, and communism seemed to be defeated, we thought the war was over. Until a new war arose—only this time it pitted Americans against each other. Called "the Culture War," it's been going on for a while with no signs of coming to an end.

A number of Christ-followers took up arms against this new enemy. Mailing lists were compiled, people recruited. Rhetoric was established, and sides were chosen. Evangelicals had a new communism to fight, filled with supposedly the same godlessness.

But if you have a war, you must also have an enemy. The two go together like fire and heat. You can't have one without the other.

Jesus was very clear that His followers only have one enemy. He faced off with that enemy as He embraced famine in the desert. Jesus' rebuke was not about the Roman rulers of the day, or religious hypocrisy, or lack of social justice. It was not about tempting Him to fall for the lies and the power the enemy promised. Those are all heavenly things…part of the spiritual war.

> If you have a war, you must also
> have an enemy. The two go together
> like fire and heat.

In this new war, the enemy did not have a face; it was an ideology. And it was deemed so terrible that a coalition had to be assembled by the leaders of the evangelical camps to fight this enemy, most surely as if they were fighting communism. The enemy was defined by their political party affiliation or their position on certain issues. It was a culture war, over earthly things.

Simply put, this Culture War is not new. Jesus faced it when He was alive, and we face it today. PC thought is not relegated solely to "liberals" outside of the church. A school of politically correct thought also resides within the church.

You see, the Culture War is mostly about power…and security. Jesus has much to say about both of those issues. He wanted His disciples then, and now, to understand that the prevailing mind-set of the day pitting the Jews against the Romans was not his concern. It still isn't.

Herod and Pilate played the politically correct game all too well. The Pharisees wanted to remain in power over their people by setting up the Romans as the bad guys. Pilate blamed everything bad that was happening on the Jewish leaders who could not control their people. Ultimately, both lifestyles would be upset if the rabble revolted. All power struggles need to create a bad guy to justify retaining their power positions.

Jesus stepped into the midst of that first-century culture war with a new way of thinking that befuddled His disciples and all those who listened to Him for any amount of time. He was a Jew, but His own religious leaders could not tolerate Him because He was a threat. Pilate could not tolerate Him because He was a threat. So, as a threat to both control groups, Jesus obviously stood for something that was beyond them. And that's His call for His followers today.

All power struggles need to
create a bad guy to justify retaining
their power positions.

Jesus is stepping into our Culture War arena in America and saying He's beyond it. Same as He did 2,000 years ago. He's a threat to both groups. And He calls out to his people to see beyond to His kingdom. To fight neither Caesar nor the Jewish leaders. The Liberals nor the Conservatives. The Republicans nor the Democrats.

Jesus confronts us to say that His followers have been co-opted by outside groups who have convinced us that the government could be changed and the country would become more like Jesus. Does that mean evangelicals should not be involved in government or the political process? No, obviously, they should. That's part of being salt and light, allowing the mind of Christ to impact legislation and provide the best government for the people.

The problem is that the Culture War-mongers co-opted evangelicals to somehow believe the government could actually become the *savior* of the American society. Thus we've replaced one Savior with another savior—the political process. In the confusion, it's all too easy to lose sight of what and whom we lift up to respect and follow.

We've replaced one Savior
with another savior.

Jesus said in the book of John, "I, when I am lifted up from the earth, will draw all men to myself" (12:32). Not if His word were lifted up. Not if His choice for a political party was lifted up. And not even if one of His disciples and best representatives was lifted up. No, He pointed to *Himself* to be lifted up. There is one very important lesson to be learned from Scripture and history: When we raise the flag higher than the cross, we have a problem.

When that happens, people get confused as to which Jesus we're talking about. Jesus divorced himself from taking sides because He knew that it only leads to an *us-versus-them* mentality. It creates trench warfare where we simply remain holed up in our foxholes of belief, preferring to lob verbal grenades and mortars into each other's camps and take on casualties.

Jesus also placed himself and His agenda above the fray, including the tricks of each camp to see whose side he took. Whether it was the Pharisees asking Him about paying taxes or when it was okay to divorce or Pilate asking if He was King of the Jews. He always responded to their verbal trickery in a way they had not considered, something more profound than their minds could imagine.

Today, some use Jesus as their excuse to denounce those who would stand against the gospel and the biblical worldview. Conversely, those all about advancing an agenda contrary to the biblical worldview see evangelicals as outdated, hypocritical, intolerant, and out of touch. Each camp views the other as the enemy. Couldn't be any colder of a war than what we have right now.

Jesus understood where the real power lay and displayed it when He washed His disciples' feet.

Those living in the first century AD had the same issues we do today: aberrant behaviors, taxes, corruption, etc. Jesus' response was to exhibit a new form of warfare—to establish the counter-culture mentality as the way to fight the Culture War. He walked the earth redefining the vocabulary of the day to suit His heavenly kingdom's purpose. His life was counter everything. Counterintuitive, countercultural. And nothing about His teachings has changed to this day.

> When we raise the flag higher
> than the cross, we have a problem.

Jesus wants His followers to lift *Him* up…and nothing else. He is not concerned with agendas of the Liberals, the Progressives, the Conservatives, or the Tea Party. He has no affiliation.

He points to Himself as the Savior with all humility and exhibits power by going to the cross. Jesus wants us to understand that the only hill to die for is Calvary. When we set up other hills, we miss the mind-set of Jesus.

If you want to fight the Culture War, leave Jesus out of it. And leave His words out of it, too. Otherwise, those who might really see Jesus in you will get confused about the gospel when you raise the flag or any cause higher than the cross.

I know Jews who are Christ-followers.
I know Muslims who are Christ-followers.
And I know Christians who aren't.

2

Diversity, Jesus-Style

Diversity is close to God's heart. Just look at nature and the people of the world. No two snowflakes are the same. Not even identical twins are identical. So, Jesus must like diversity, too, right? Wrong.

Simply put, the biblical notion of diversity is recognizing the uniqueness of creation (which includes mankind). Political correctness interprets diversity as justifying behaviors that Jesus could not accept. It's important to distinguish between diversity as part of natural law, and therefore part of God's plan, and man's attempts to redefine diversity to contradict the laws of creation and nature.

PC equates diversity with a blanket acceptance of lifestyles. In fact, *diversity* has become one of the "darlings" of the politically correct lexicon. Differences, all differences, are not only okay, but to be celebrated. Jesus throws a wet blanket on that thinking with statements like, "What comes out of a man is what makes him unclean. For from within, out of men's hearts, come evil thoughts, sexual immorality, theft, murder, adultery, greed, malice, deceit, lewdness, envy, slander, arrogance and folly. All these evils come from inside and make a man unclean" (Mark 7:21–23).

Political correctness interprets diversity as inclusiveness. Yet, with that passage from the book of Mark, Jesus has just excluded a bunch of people from the kingdom of God. Today that thinking would get Him in trouble with the PC police.

The truth is, Jesus was anything but inclusive. He even said, "Wide is the gate and broad is the road that leads to destruction, and many enter through it. But small is the gate and narrow the road that leads to life" (Matthew 7:13–14). Those words don't sound too inclusive to me, and they didn't sound that way either back when He walked the earth. In fact, the PC police of His day, the Pharisees, got really upset at Jesus when He made comments like that.

> Political correctness interprets diversity as inclusiveness. Jesus was anything but inclusive.

The only thing Jesus was inclusive about was His Father's love for mankind. He reminded people that He was the visible expression of God the Father's love for the human race by being the payment for man's sin.

Oops. There's that word *sin*. Diversity has a problem with that word since it infers that what Jesus described as making men unclean were lifestyles and attitudes that separated them from God. Jesus does not accept the inclusiveness of diversity when it comes to accepting all lifestyles and all roads leading in the same direction toward God. When Jesus said, "I am the way and the truth and the life. No one comes to the Father except through me" (John 14:6), He was about as exclusive as it gets. Frankly, it's a rather troubling statement.

In our current politically correct climate, the notion of exclusivity is antithetical to the concept of diversity. The two cannot get along. Yet diversity's mantra is, "Why can't we all just get along?"

Jesus came along to say, well, that we all can't get along. That's the problem. Which is why He claimed that God sent Him to die. Man had to first get along with God before he was able to get along with his fellow humans.

Interestingly, diversity would exclude the Jesus of the New Testament because of His rather exclusive position on many things like describing the road to God as being narrow and not wide, pointing to Himself as absolute truth incarnate, having the authority to forgive sin, etc. And, in doing so, would remove the one thing (Jesus) that actually would satisfy what PC wants to accomplish!

Leave it up to us humans to get it all backward.

Our minds are
not repositories for
someone else's garbage.

3

March of the Trojan Horses

I always liked ancient history, especially reading about the great military campaigns of Caesar in the Gallic Wars, the Greeks and their Peloponnesian Wars, and Alexander the Great's conquests, to name a few.

My favorite general was Hannibal. Anyone who can spend sixteen years in Italy fighting the Romans on elephants and crossing mountains with a bunch of pachyderms has my vote. You really had to be a strategist in those days to win wars. No smart bombs, drones, or naval warfare.

One of my favorite stories of those ancient battles involved the use of the Trojan horse. Now that was smart. It sure saved a lot of time fighting to get into the city of Troy. Imagine, getting your enemy to think he's getting a gift when he's really letting in what will ultimately defeat him.

How neat.

How deadly.

In this generation, I get the feeling history is repeating itself.

Certain influences have been so subtle, so cloaked in popular causes that we've failed to recognize them for what they are. The enemy is not obvious. He comes as a wolf in sheep's clothing. There are no invading barbarian hordes, no wild-eyed reprobates lurking in the shadows curling their mustaches. And because we have not seen them for what they are, we've readily embraced these influences as acceptable manners of expression. They look like gifts, but once we let them in our gates, we're attacked.

One of the most heinous of the Trojan horses is the PC mantra of an amoral society. There is no more right or wrong in setting standards of morality because there is no one truth. No cause, no effect. Our kids are paying the price of sexual identity confusion, bullying in record numbers, and parental distraction.

There is no more right or wrong in
setting standards of morality because there
is no one truth. No cause, no effect.

I became acutely aware of this scenario in a rather strange way— by shopping with my daughter some 8–10 years ago. Sounds rather innocent, but a closer look revealed something more insidious.

While we were at a mall, my daughter asked to go into a very hip, fashionable store for teens to buy a shirt. It must have been more than 20 years since I'd set foot in that store. As I entered, I stopped dead in my tracks. I thought I was in the wrong store— that I'd walked into an X-rated video establishment. Pictures of half-naked young women (probably not much older than my daughter) lying on top of equally undressed young men adorned the walls.

After spending my life in marketing and communication, there was no mistaking what those images and messages were meant to convey. They were very clear—our culture has sacrificed the innocence of our youth on the altar of sexual glorification. It's no longer about selling clothes; it's more about selling our souls. We decry the way our wives and daughters are disparaged over their body images and seen as sexual objects, yet promulgate the very lifestyles and clothing lines that lead to the thing we denounce. We have become a schizophrenic society.

It's no longer about selling clothes; it's more about selling our souls.

But wait, the story did not end there.

My daughter knew me all too well. She knew I'd likely say something and not merely slip away into the night, momentarily decrying the decadence of the situation and then doing nothing. As I stood in the line waiting to pay for the shirt, I grew madder by the minute. Let's just call it righteous indignation.

As I approached the counter to pay, I observed the young man and young woman who were standing there to serve us. They were probably around 19 or 20 years old. I placed the shirt on the counter and then informed the young man that I was really offended by the display on the walls. "Please pass my comments on to the manager," I insisted.

Of course, I didn't stop there, even though my daughter, embarrassed by my approach, was turning quite red.

I asked the young man, "How do you feel about working in this environment, particularly working alongside a young lady?"

Then I asked her, "How do you feel about all of this? Are you offended, even a little bit? Does this promote the wholesome way in which you'd like to be perceived by the young man working alongside you?"

I guess it was the journalist in me that needed to ask the obvious questions, as I saw them.

As my daughter muttered under her breath, "Dad, they don't care," the young man eyed me. "I wish my father cared as much," he said.

That was his exact quote. I'll never forget it.

As we left the store, my daughter sighed. "You know, he had to say that."

"No," I replied, "he could have said any number of things, like, 'I'll tell my manager.' "

To this day I'm convinced he said what he said because it was on his heart to say it.

Jesus said that out of the heart come the issues of life. And I suspect that, in this young man's heart, rarely did he see evidence of a man standing up for what he believed to protect his child from the attack of this Trojan horse.

Jesus is so at odds with our culture and, at times, even the church as we casually accept society's hell-bent inclination toward self-aggrandizement over altruism, greed in the midst of plenty, a growing dishonesty in personal relationships, the disintegration of marriage, decreasing lack of civility, and yes, the increasing moral ambivalence that suffocates our youth with sexual indulgence beyond their ability to handle it or even understand it.

Yes, Jesus has something to say to each of us about these issues. But we must listen closely to His words and not spin them to suit the prevailing moral climate brought about by political correctness.

The Trojan horse in this respect is what we have allowed into our minds and homes as the way in which we sell products. It's no longer about the product, but the message embodied by that product. The classic example is Harley Davidson motorcycles. Harley commercials do not depict what's good about the bike, but the freedom it gives to the owner. The unspoken message is that owning a Harley bike is all about independence and self-expression.

In that clothing store, maybe the message was about sexual revolution or that young people have a prevailing mind-set of openness toward sex. Or maybe it was all about sameness and androgyny. Who knows?

I do know that messages are intentional, and the intent is to sneak into our souls so we accept a particular mind-set as the way our culture now is.

Jesus asks us to be counterculturalists. We are to challenge the prevailing mind-sets that are antithetical to how Jesus wants us to relate to each other and to think of each other.

I'm reminded of one of my favorite quotes of Dr. Francis Schaeffer, celebrated Christian apologist/author, who said:

> The Christian must resist the spirit of the world in the form it takes in his generation. He must understand what confronts him antagonistically in history. Otherwise, he simply becomes a museum piece and not a living warrior for Christ.[1]

A museum piece is a reminder of the past that sits on a shelf and collects dust. People pass by it and comment on how nice it may look and how relevant it was back then, but it has no real importance in the present.

I don't know about you, but I don't want to be a museum piece.

So, if you seem to be collecting dust, you might want to do something about it.

Watch what gift you accept from the culture. It may look nice, but it could be a Trojan horse.

When we cower to those forces
in our culture that tell us to rename our
symbols because someone might be
"insulted" because they do not believe
similarly, they are creating fear
and division. Not tolerance.

4

Renaming Christmas

C hristmas. It conjures up a boatload of memories for many
people. Some good. Some not.

But there's always one thing you can count on at Christmas
that's as prominent as Santa and the songs of the season—political
correctness.

It's the time of year when the PC police experience their peren-
nial angst about the symbols of Christmas and will not rest until
all vestige of the reason for the season is expunged from the marketplace. Somehow we've allowed these self-appointed gatekeepers
of American traditions to scare us into renaming Christmas, the
Christmas tree, our greetings to each other, and who knows what
else. And don't forget about the crèche…that terribly offensive display that arouses so much ire among some groups that they take
city governments to court to have those displays removed from the
public square.

So what's all this have to do with Jesus?

To answer that, it might be helpful first to provide some background information on political correctness. And don't just take my

word for it. Check this out for yourself. Most people are not aware of the Marxist roots of political correctness that started in Europe in the 1920s as a subtle way to redefine language and symbols of culture in Marxist terms.

Initially, the idea was to pit the working class against the ruling class, which did not take very much effort back in the early twentieth century, given the conditions in Europe after the First World War. This new ideology took hold in Europe and eventually was exported to America.

Under the guise of equality and tolerance, the true intent of the PC movement was to create an *us-versus-them* mentality by pitting people against each other—rich against poor, male against female, victims against their oppressors. The idea was to create artificial rifts and paranoia between groups.

> The true intent of the PC movement
> was to create an *us-versus-them*
> mentality by pitting people
> against each other.

The PC goal was and is to identify certain minority groups (not necessarily ethnic, but the poor and oppressed at first) who would be the good guys because they were kept at bay by the ruling classes (the bad guys), which were primarily white and wealthy in Europe. Since many of the proponents of this new ideology were atheists, they had to include religion, particularly Christianity, as another one of the antagonists in the class struggle since religion was seen as a tool of the wealthy, ruling class. Judeo-Christian thought was particularly singled out for deconstruction because its symbols and theology were so antithetical to Marxist thinking.

Of course, we all know where Marxist thinking took us in the twentieth century…to Stalinist Russia, communist China, and the killing fields of the Khmer Rouge of Cambodia.

Eventually, that ideology came to America, where the fertile ground of the 1960s counterculture, radical movements provided the right conditions to fuel the growth of the PC movement. There were ready-made antagonists and protagonists—the necessary ingredients to a good Marxist revolution…or the establishment of a politically correct movement.

I'll stop there with the history lesson. But a little background was necessary because otherwise it's a long leap from Marxism to why we now say "happy holidays" and renamed Christmas trees to holiday trees. However, let me be very clear: Many well-meaning-people have a politically correct mind-set, but they are no more Marxist than me.

The real faith issue is that Jesus asked us to render unto Caesar what was his and to God what is His. That quote from Mark 12:17 was in the context of the Pharisees trying to corner Jesus into the politically incorrect answer of suggesting that His followers should not pay taxes. They were trying to get Jesus to pit the Jews against the Romans; their version of God versus the Roman system of many gods. Jesus came back at them with something so entirely different that the logic of it baffled His tempters.

Jesus asked us to render unto Caesar what was his and to God what is His.

Not much has changed over the years. That is still the battle today. Political correctness needs good guys and bad guys to pit against each other, but Jesus comes along and says that the state is not our enemy and neither is the ruling class, another group of people, the wealthy, the poor, etc. He obliterates the *us-versus-them* mentality that is part of the politically correct agenda.

God is bigger than the state, which exists only by God's grace and design. Its power is limited. It cannot rule over the longing of the human spirit that cries out for freedom. Did you ever wonder where the idea behind "life, liberty and the pursuit of happiness" came from? Not from *The Communist Manifesto*.

Simply, PC cannot tolerate the notion of God in the public square because it is scared of God.

When the state or some other group seeks to control what we think, what we say, and creates fear to say what is on our minds and to question authority, and attempts to usurp the role of God in our lives, that is the beginning of totalitarianism. When we cower to those forces in our culture that tell us to rename our symbols because someone might be "insulted" because they do not believe similarly, they are creating fear and division. Not tolerance.

When my daughter was perhaps five or six, we were driving by our town hall where a crèche, a menorah, and a Santa were exhibited. Of course, political correctness would prefer to have us remove the crèche and menorah. Fortunately, that did not happen.

The crèche was familiar to my daughter, as was Santa. But not the menorah. So she asked me what the menorah was. I then had the privilege of using that symbol as a teaching opportunity to explain the story of the miracle of how one day's worth of oil lasted for eight, and then how the Maccabees, with God's help, freed their people from their oppressors. I relished the opportunity to remove some of the mystery from what had been, up to that point, unknown to my daughter.

You see, when you remove the mystery from something unknown, fear and misunderstanding wane. And that is the beginning of tolerance. Awareness and education mitigates intolerance. Political correctness encourages disinformation.

When you remove the mystery
from something unknown, fear and
misunderstanding wane.

Also, the freedom to display our symbols and discuss our heritages provides a basis for understanding the greatness of our country. Hiding them encourages ignorance. And we all know what ignorance breeds. Racism. Hate. Suspicion.

Have you ever wondered why our society seems to be more divided than before? More suspicious of each other than ever? Why there is more white-collar crime? More hate crimes? All these issues surface as a natural progression of the stripping away of our biblical foundations of respect for the individual and adhering to a moral code beyond ourselves. The very thing that builds tolerance is being systematically deleted from our public square in the name of political correctness.

We have turned off the lights slowly, and now it's getting dark. Political correctness wants to keep us in the dark. It attempts to hide that which is obvious and plainly visible and redefine what we believe. It's done subtly, but done nonetheless.

Jesus steps into the middle of all this and says what He did 2,000 years ago: Render to Caesar what's his and to God what's His. He wants us to go beyond the cultural rivalry fostered by political correctness and simply be lights to truth.

Light always dispels darkness. Faith demands honesty. It fosters freedom and despises intolerance. It demands an ethic beyond our ability to live it and gives us boundaries for our safety. It also tells a government that it exists for the people, not for itself. And, to the chagrin of many, it tells us that we are not gods.

He wants us to go beyond the cultural
rivalry fostered by political correctness
and simply be lights to truth.

The next Christmas season, when you hear the same old politically correct rhetoric, remember that by allowing those messages to control your life, you are participating in one of the great ruses being perpetrated on the American people.

Instead, choose to opt out of intellectual dishonesty. Choose light instead of darkness. Jesus said He was the light of the world.

I'd rather listen to Jesus. He died for me. PC wants me to die for it. The choice is simple.

"BE THOU MY VISION"

Be Thou my Vision, O Lord of my heart;
Naught be all else to me, save that Thou art;
Thou my best Thought, by day or by night,
Waking or sleeping, Thy presence my light.

Be Thou my Wisdom, and Thou my true Word;
I ever with Thee and Thou with me, Lord;
Thou my great Father, I Thy true son;
Thou in me dwelling, and I with Thee one.

Be Thou my battle Shield, Sword for the fight;
Be Thou my Dignity, Thou my Delight
Thou my soul's Shelter, Thou my high Tow'r:
Raise Thou me heave'nward, O Pow'r of my pow'r.

Riches I heed not, nor man's empty praise,
Thou mine inheritance, now and always:
Thou and Thou only, first in my heart
High King of Heaven, my Treasure Thou art.

High King of heaven, my victory won,
May I reach heaven's joys, O bright heav'n's Sun!
Heart of my own heart, whate'er befall,
Still be my Vision, O Ruler of all.

—Original Old Irish text attributed to
Saint Dallán Forgaill, sixth century

Righteousness without tears
is arrogance. I'm afraid the world
has seen too much of our righteousness
and too few of our tears.

5

Common
Ground

Have you ever heard the adage that you should never discuss religion and politics in certain social circumstances? Well, a few years ago, it was both politics and religion that enabled me to be invited to Washington, DC, to meet with some leaders of a particular political party and one of their think tanks.

The events leading up to that invitation were pretty interesting. In 2004 I had been involved in a campaign called *Redeem the Vote*, which encouraged young people of faith to register to vote. The campaign was rather successful in its effort to have young men and women download voter registration forms. It also garnered lots of national press for its chief spokesperson and founder, as well as some artists we had enlisted to help through a number of public service announcements they voiced that I had written, produced, and cleared on radio stations nationwide.

We had so much success in that endeavor that we (the founder and I) were invited to meet with some leaders of this particular party because they said we were the only non-strident evangelicals they knew. That was a sad indictment—either of the evangelicals they had met or of themselves, for never taking the time to associate with evangelicals. Or maybe it was a little bit of both. However, isn't it like most of us, who rarely hang out with people whose worldviews are dramatically different from our own?

If we're Christ-followers, Jesus prefers that we choose to be around those who are different from us. Isolating ourselves only with those with whom we agree on everything is so opposite of how Jesus interacted and intersected with people unlike Him, the social outcasts of his day.

A Jew associating with a Samaritan woman was forbidden (John 4). A religious leader associating with a prostitute or a leper would have made that leader unclean. The social calendars of many people during that period were pretty predetermined.

Jesus prefers that we choose
to be around those who are
different from us.

In our case, the people we met in DC rarely intersected with Christ-followers…much like a thief wouldn't call a cop to help him break into someone's home. If two groups are busy going in opposite political and cultural directions, they rarely take the time to consider there may be some reason to intersect with each other. Either group might consider the other the leper of their world.

Which is sad, because our interaction in DC resulted in wonderful new friendships between several of those individuals whose lives would have been untouched by mine, and vice versa, had we not decided to go outside of ourselves to find the other.

During one of our meetings in a rather nice home in Georgetown, we answered questions about how best to work with evangelicals on issues that supposedly divided us, such as abortion, immigration, gay rights, etc.

At one point, one individual asked me, "What is the evangelical middle ground on abortion?"

"There really is none," I replied. "One cannot have a middle ground on the sanctity-of-life issue, as it's firmly grounded in an inviolate law of God about when life begins and who can determine a disturbance in its continuum."

At that point, the man threw his arms in the air. "See, there's no talking with you evangelicals, because you refuse to discuss things like this!"

I replied kindly that he was asking me the wrong question. "It's not about finding the middle ground to when life begins and when it's okay to summarily take that life," I told him. "The better question would be how to find common ground, not middle ground." I took a breath and went on. "Middle ground suggests that we compromise on something we have no right in doing—violating our conscience and our understanding of God's Word. That's not finding middle ground; that's a sellout. Or intellectual dishonesty, at best."

Middle ground suggests that we compromise on something we have no right in doing—violating our conscience and our understanding of God's Word.

I continued to say that the higher ground is trying to find common ground so that even if we may not agree on a particular issue, we can still strive to find what we can agree on that satisfies both of our positions. "Can we honestly work to both minimize the opportunity for abortion and still protect someone's right under the Constitution?" I asked him. "And still respect each other's positions while maintaining a civil discourse with each other?"

Even if we may not agree on a particular issue,
we can still strive to find what we can agree on
that satisfies *both* of our positions.

I suggested, "So, as good management strategy would dictate, we should start at the end result of our desired goal. In this case, the obvious common ground is to reduce the number of abortions as much as possible, if not entirely. Most evangelicals would rather see fewer abortions each year than seeing no reduction, year in and year out. A platform of attrition is one way to address the issue and would allow for pro-life people from either party to speak into the issue and forge a model that can work."

He looked surprised and intrigued.

The result of that evening's very interesting interaction was that I was retained to help craft some understanding of how evangelicals think on certain issues and what could be common ground between the two groups. A white paper was published that did find that common ground on some key social issues, thereby creating more of a dialogue between us that even allowed God to show up in the discussion.

Political correctness might suggest we leave God and the Bible out of the discussion when discussing politics. After all, the two are known for not mixing well.

But, as a Christ-follower, my work is simply to show up in scenarios that might allow His presence a place at the table. If I recuse myself from the discussions because I have an allegiance to one idea over another, one political expression over another, my opinion will never be heard. If I never enter into a foreign environment emotionally and intellectually, I will never expose others to what I believe. And I will never know what others believe so I can then better understand how to make a cogent defense of the gospel, as we are instructed. That's also called mission work. In my opinion, mission work is not relegated to a geographical point on a map.

As a Christ-follower, my work is simply
to show up in scenarios that might allow
His presence a place at the table.

Being a Christ-follower is all about finding that common ground with everyone. Jesus did that exceptionally well. The Samaritan woman at the well in John 4 is a good case in point. The neat thing about this story is that Jesus went out of His way to find someone whom society said He should avoid, or disregard. Maybe not unlike the people I met and their aversion to Christ-followers.

I realize many people run from evangelicals because they only know what we stand against, not what we stand for.

Like the woman at the well, I suspect my new friends feared that an association with evangelicals would be more about judgment and condemnation than forgiveness. They probably see that more often than they see the Mother Teresa kind of love, and that may cloud their thinking. I get it.

But the Bible is clear that Jesus does not condemn, and neither should we. The most famous passage in all of Scripture may be John 3:16, which speaks of God's love for man by sending His Son to die for us. The next verse says, "For God did not send his Son into the world to condemn the world, but to save the world through him." We see that exhibited plainly in His dealing with the woman at the well (John 4) and the woman caught in adultery (John 8). He forgave both and asked them to not continue in their sin. But He didn't chide them for their sin, nor condemn them. He allowed Himself to intersect with their lives to show them God's love and reorient their focus that had been clouded by the religious thinking they were accustomed to.

He didn't chide them for their sin, nor
condemn them. He allowed Himself to
intersect with their lives.

Neither did Jesus pretend their sin wasn't obvious. But bringing a person face to face with their sin is the work of the Holy Spirit. It is the Holy Spirit who convicts (John 16:7–11). Note it says He *convicts,* not condemns. Neither Jesus nor the Holy Spirit condemn people. Jesus confronted sin in a loving manner. Conviction does not leave love out of the equation, whereas condemnation leaves no room for love. Conviction is born of love; condemnation from no compassion.

Some of God's so-called representatives are too quick to condemn because they misunderstand God's love and their role in the kingdom. It's a hard thing to handle absolute truth. For some, it makes us hard, unloving, and unable to find common ground.

Isaiah 1:18 says, "'Come now, let us reason together,' says the Lord." Unreasonable people, whether right or wrong, hardly ever make headway on tough issues.

For others, it illumines our weaknesses and drives us to find that common ground with others, sometimes through tears. My good friend Steve Brown says that righteousness without tears is arrogance. I'm afraid the world has seen too much of our righteousness and too little of our tears. I bet Jesus spoke with the woman at the well and the woman caught in adultery with compassion. He may have even gotten moist in the eyes when He understood their situation.

I'm afraid the world has seen too much of our
righteousness and too little of our tears.

So, my time in DC with my newfound friends once again showed me that my role is to find a way to help all people find that common ground between themselves and God. People who may be very different from me politically are really much the same as me in so many other ways. It just takes some time to look for the commonality between us. That's called *communication*.

And when communication happens, our role as defined in 2 Corinthians 5:18–20 will jump out at us—that we are to reestablish friendship between others and God and act as His ambassadors. That takes finding the common ground.

All this is from God, who reconciled us to himself through Christ and gave us the ministry of reconciliation: that God was reconciling the world to himself in Christ, not counting people's sins against them. And he has committed to us the message of reconciliation. We are therefore Christ's ambassadors, as though God were making his appeal through us. We implore you on Christ's behalf: Be reconciled to God.

—2 Corinthians 5:18–20

We now look for truth
in dung heaps.

6

Of Mice
and Media

I'm a card-carrying member of the media. I've spent my life and career in New York and worked with some very talented broadcasters, writers, producers, and journalists.

I earned my degree in Journalism from Boston University and then put it to use upon graduation in launching a magazine for the New York area Christian community. It was a wonderful learning experience that ultimately led to the entrée to my career in broadcasting the following year.

During the year in between the launch of the magazine and my first job in broadcasting, I developed a biblical working definition of my profession. This was the basis of my thesis for an urban theological one-year program I was involved in through New York Seminary with 12 other guys from around the country. Well-known cross-cultural expert and church planter Bill Iverson led this group.

For this thesis, I went back to the original Greek language to see what words were used to describe concepts of communication. Interestingly, the words most often used were *logos* and *koinonia*. These

Greek words describe the highest form of communication (Jesus was referred to as the Logos) in the context of community.

In effect, the communicator seeks to create a common link between himself and his audience with the highest principles of logic and accuracy. It is *deductive* in its reasoning and approach.

There's a measure of intellectual honesty because you state what is because it's obvious. And if it's not so obvious, you do your best to describe what you're seeing—not what you want to see. Which led me to my definition of journalism: "To illumine what others cannot see."

Now, let's turn the page to where we've found ourselves in our current politically correct world that asks us to not state the obvious because it might offend someone or rubs a certain group of people the wrong way. In a strange twist on art imitating life, this thinking reminds me of the *Invasion of the Body Snatchers,* that classic sci-fi film of the 1950s where seed pods land on earth and take over the entire personas of people when they're asleep. Then they turn into robotic replicas of the people whose identities they assume, void of passion, independent thinking, feelings, or emotion. Everyone is the same…except the way they look.

In a similar way, I think our media has been taken over by those seed pods. Something has come over these communicators…has invaded their thinking so they no longer seek to define the obvious with accuracy of interpretation. More and more, it seems as if some journalists embrace the *inductive* approach: "If it's not there, I'll inject it into the story."

Some journalists embrace the
inductive approach: "If it's not there,
I'll inject it into the story."

Media personalities have now become seething advocates of ideology, not truth. Their mantra seems to be: "State your position.

Defend it regardless of whether it's true or not, or even applicable to the situation. Argue to make yourself heard. Not because you have something to say, but because you have nothing to say."

Whether liberal or conservative, it's equally distasteful. This is beyond partisan anything.

Our media is in danger of embracing the same noblesse oblige attitude toward the masses as the leadership in Washington has. This attitude is insulting. The hoi poloi can no longer figure out anything for themselves. We now have to put up with the self-appointed interpreters of what is apparent. We are treated as if people are fragile, all ideas are equal, and some contemporary thought is only as chic as those who promulgate it. It's the PC thinking de jour: It need not be accurate nor exhibit common sense, just be popular.

Instead of searching for truth in the struggle with reality, we turn to the expedient and the sound bite. One needn't be intelligent, just photogenic or famous. Warhol's 15 minutes of fame has become an extended period of time until the public vomits everything it's been told to swallow.

The PC thinking de jour:
It needn't be accurate nor exhibit
common sense, just be popular.

Tragically, we now look for truth in dung heaps. We stick our hand in the muck, pull it out and hold up what we've grabbed, admire it, then declare it relevant and to be believed. And when all those who have not drunk the Kool-Aid and still have a modicum of common sense look at it in disbelief and say openly, "It's just a pile of dung"—it's hard to refrain from using the more expletive synonym here—those who disagree are excoriated because they are not in lockstep with the PC thought of the day that truth no longer matters. Or even exists. The obvious is no longer obvious, as to state the obvious would fly in the face of the approved political-speak of the day advocated by the self-appointed gatekeepers of the American lexicon.

But that's not new. Jesus had to confront His version of the media elite of His day, those who were the communicators of all that was supposed to be evident and true to the masses in need of explanations. These were the self-proclaimed righteous religious rulers who acted as the journalists who were more interested in sustaining their versions of what was than telling people the truth.

We now look for truth
in dung heaps.

Jesus steps into this arena and begins to help people see beyond the political-speak to what is real in the kingdom of God. In the Sermon on the Mount, Jesus used that platform to interpret life and truth in another language than what everyone traditionally heard from the communicators of the day. He certainly fit my definition of the journalist—the one who can illumine what others cannot see. He interpreted how to live life in the "blessed are you" comments about the meek, the poor in spirit, the hungry, etc.

This was a new kind of truth, stripped of the politically correct speak of His day because it went beyond all that rhetoric. It stated things that neither Caesar nor the ruling Jewish elite had a grasp of. Jesus redefined the ground rules and brought new definition to life's experiences.

Jesus is still doing that today. He wants to redefine the PC speak of our day so we no longer have to scrounge in dung heaps to find truth like much of our media asks us to do. He said He was the truth and went on to say that the truth would set you free (John 8:32).

He also asks us to be perfect, as our heavenly Father is perfect (Matthew 5:48). Interestingly, he states this at the end of the section about loving our enemies because there's nothing harder than forgiving the people who want to harm you. So he picks the hardest thing for us to humanly do in order to be perfect. Why do you think He did that? To show that we simply cannot be perfect. He points us to the need and then says He will be the One to help us meet that need.

Jesus redefined the ground rules
and brought new definition to
life's experiences.

The good news is that we can find freedom in that truth when we find Jesus.

All the politically correct speak of the day that asks us to accept absurdity as reality flies in the face of the words of Jesus. He is our Logos, the highest form of truth and logic, and He asks each of us to simply look at life through the grid He provided. When we do, we find freedom, rest, love, forgiveness, and charity. These are the fruit of a life hidden in His truth.

So, when the PC speak of the day asks us to accept whatever it has pulled from the dung heap, let's just say what it is. And that it smells.

The aroma that Jesus leaves us with when He presents His truth is sweet. It's filled with peace and grace.

The world offers us dung. Jesus offers us the aroma of life. Choose wisely.

For our entertainment,
we now glorify the villains
and vilify the glorious.

7

The Indigestion
of Entertainment

I was flipping through the zillions of channels on my television set the other day just to see what's available. I do that from time to time as an exercise in keeping myself culturally aware.

At least that's my excuse for doing it. It drives my wife nuts, so I try to do it when she's not around or on another TV set in the house. Sometimes my dog will join me, and she's okay with that. The dog, that is. My wife would probably not approve of doing that in front of our dog!

But I'm a curious guy, so I enjoy seeing what's out there that I might be missing. Most of the time, after scanning for a few minutes, it's apparent I'm not missing anything! Sometimes I'm pleasantly surprised. More often, I'm disappointed at what the public is being fed as entertainment.

I know I'm getting older. So is it just me, or does it seem like our entertainment was once taken more seriously? Great comedy. Engaging drama. Real news.

There's a fascinating correlation between how we nourish and satisfy the part of us that appreciates and even requires a creative interaction with our environments, such as our entertainment choices and our own personal growth as individuals. How we ultimately treat each other is an outward expression of how we inwardly feel about ourselves. And how we feel about ourselves and how we understand our world is often a function of what we "ingest" in our entertainment choices and the news we consume.

The kind of programming we ingest into our minds will often dictate what we eliminate from our mouths. A diet of information that denigrates rather than elevates the human spirit will find its way out in what we say and do.

If we only expose ourselves to the news that fits our worldview, then we will only have a worldview that compounds what we already believe. The more entertainment choices we have *can* reinforce entrenched positions, rather than expanding and illuminating perspectives beyond ourselves. We can expose ourselves to 24 hours of sameness all day long.

If we want *only* to hear a conservative spin on events and issues, we are encouraged to turn to FOX News. If we want *only* a liberal spin, we are told to turn to MSNBC or CNN. With the plethora of options, rather than becoming more liberal in the classic sense of broad-mindedness to appreciate a variety of worldviews, we've become more narrow-minded and closed to other thoughts and ideas.

And when that happens, we see that acted out in our culture. There is more fear. More insecurity. More lack of civility.

With the plethora of options, we've become more narrow-minded and closed to other thoughts and ideas.

Why has this happened?

I believe the PC notion to eliminate the idea of absolutes has contributed to this downfall. If there is no right and wrong, everyone's opinions and ideas are as true and valuable to society as everyone else's.

Once we eliminate the notion of what's good or bad, the slippery slope of what people will do and tolerate becomes more acceptable. For example, as we experience the surge of "surreality shows," as I call them (reality shows are not reality. They are scripted fictional expressions of life), we have fallen in love with what is not actually true. We think it's true because we call them *reality* shows, but we know better.

Or do we?

As a trained journalist, I always understood my job to observe and interpret the news. Unfortunately, that's all changed, it seems. We've exchanged information and observation for titillation. We've become a nation of voyeurs, people who are content to sit and gawk at others' lives. We no longer have any sense of shame, because we're told there's nothing to be ashamed of anymore.

> We've exchanged information
> and observation for titillation.
> We've become a nation of voyeurs,
> people who are content to sit and
> gawk at others' lives.

So we are content to live vicariously through others, regardless of how insipid, mean, banal, or fruitless the participants are or what they do. Fame is to be celebrated above all else. We can watch others cheat on their spouses, have children out of wedlock, have meltdowns in their homes, and denigrate others openly and joyously. Then awards are handed out to the people and shows that celebrate all these things.

This is the new entertainment. It appeals to the lowest common denominator or prurient interest in man rather than aspiring to explore our higher, more noble essence with content that reaches for the stars. Now we glorify the villains, and vilify the glorious. We create celebrities of those who have no gift, no talent, no redeeming elements to their lives other than to belittle others and themselves in the process.

> We glorify the villains,
> and vilify the glorious.

A constant diet of the type of entertainment we consume kicks in the desire to be like those we emulate. If we feed on programs that belittle or breed insecurity, we can embrace those attributes, becoming insecure and belittling ourselves. As we unknowingly internalize the character qualities uplifted, they ultimately come out in our behavior.

Our society is now beginning to pay the price. We've ingested all we can, and it's time for the messy elimination process. What is coming out is a smelly form of excrement.

We've gorged ourselves on what is destructive and violent and have created a culture of violence. Because we've laughed at the shows that belittle and denigrate, there are more incidents of acting-out scenarios of bullying and meanness in the public square than ever before.

We've decided it's okay to put on pedestals those who cheat, connive to get ahead, or lie to their spouses and friends. But we watch and wonder why our families are disintegrating, leaving behind the carnage of broken children. Then we ponder anew when those broken children grow up and decide to act out their fear and insecurity with violence—sometimes with their fists, but all too often with a handy weapon of choice. The tragic results of what our culture has produced are littered around us.

Though we have aimed for the lowest common denominator of entertainment, we moan when we find that played out in our culture as to how people actually treat each other. And how our businesses treat their customers.

> Though we have aimed for the lowest common
> denominator of entertainment, we moan when
> we find that played out in our culture as to how
> people actually treat each other.

The apostle Paul knew all too well the indigestion of entertainment when he told us: "Whatever is true, whatever is noble, whatever is right, whatever is pure, whatever is lovely, whatever is admirable—if anything is excellent or praiseworthy—think about such things" (Philippians 4:8). He understood this universal truth: What goes in will ultimately come out.

I learned long ago that my mind doesn't have to be a repository for someone else's garbage. Nor should yours be. We reap what we sow.

So watch out what entertains you. The drama you vicariously see and enjoy on the screen may one day be yours experientially to share in.

Truth is dangerous because
it is contagious.

8

The Obvious Will Become Obvious

When I was a kid, I'd often sit with my father watching the old TV series *The Untouchables*. It starred Robert Stack as Elliott Ness, the leader of a group of FBI G-men who fought organized crime. Seems like most of the bad guys had names similar to mine—they all ended in a vowel, and they spoke the same language of my family. I'm a first generation Italian-American (both my parents were born in Italy). My paternal grandparents lived with us, as well. So, we were *very* Italian, complete with a chicken coop my grandfather built, the wine cellar, and the all-day family fests that regular people called Sunday lunch.

Anyway, during this one episode that introduced yet another criminal to the story line with an Italian surname, my father loudly proclaimed his displeasure as to why everyone had to be of Italian origin. To which I replied once, "Dad, probably because they were."

What can you say to that?

Today's "bad guys" come in a different form. If you're looking for extremists or terrorists, they can be from any nationality. It's now more about ideology than ethnicity. Which makes it even more dangerous. Recently, certain law enforcement authorities have been infiltrating extremist Islamic groups that may have potential ties to terrorist activity, and the outcry of profiling is heard nationwide. In light of 9-11 and other acts of terrorism advocated by spokespersons of radical Islam, government surveillance of these groups has increased. I mean, where else are you going to look first?

When all the Mafia family bosses were being targeted for surveillance, the FBI was not wiretapping local hangouts of the Daughters of the American Revolution. I suspect there may be some of you who are not familiar with this unique sorority of flag-waving, mom and apple-pie descendants of those who fought in the Revolutionary War, and who could not be further from the stereotypical Mafiosi persona.

An unfortunate result of malevolent behavior of those from various ethnic backgrounds can often lead to stereotypes. And those stereotypes lead to other unfortunate incidents, sometimes at the expense of the innocent.

So today, the politically correct police are like my father, who felt offended because people were simply stating the obvious—most of the organized crime bosses were Italian. Those names weren't made up. There was no plot to defame those of Italian heritage. But, in our current PC world, we are told to stay away from offending anyone, regardless of what is obvious or even true. It seems that certain groups of people seemingly can enjoy the same endangered species status of the white tiger or humpback whale. Entire people groups or ideologies have been declared "no critique zones."

In our current PC world, we are told to stay away from offending anyone, regardless of what is obvious or even true.

That's called "tolerance." But is it really tolerance?

For example, if you're a high-profile individual and hold to a traditional view of marriage of one woman, one man and somehow state that, you may be the brunt of the wrath of certain gay community activists or media icons simply because of your belief. You haven't said anything disparaging about what you don't believe or about anyone who may not believe what you do. You have only stated what you do believe. Well, you'd think that you just formed a welcoming committee for Al-Qaeda in your community.

Disagreement is no longer seen as an opportunity for constructive dialogue. Instead, some would consider it tantamount to a "hate crime."

Tolerance is no longer two sides of a coin. It's been redefined and turned into the suppression of opinion by the ones who seem to hold the politically correct power. Now, what good does that do? Who does that protect?

> Disagreement is no longer seen as an opportunity for constructive dialogue.

Political correctness would prefer to turn a blind eye toward the obvious for fear of offending people. Just as most of the members of the Mafia are Italian, and members of the Russian mob are, well, Russian, and most of the Islamic extremists are Muslims. You cannot escape the obvious. But stating it could get you in trouble.

Just like it did with Jesus when He encountered similar situations. He would state the obvious all the time. Like when He confronted the Pharisees and said that they were like whitewashed tombs because their words sounded high and mighty but they had no love inside of them for the people (Matthew 23:27–28).

When He healed individuals on the Sabbath (Matthew 12:9–14) or stated that He was God and could give life (John 6:39), He was going against the PC status of His day. Those in power could not allow those kinds of comments from Jesus to be promulgated among the people. It could be infectious.

Truth is dangerous because it is contagious.

Why do you think there's so much anger and argumentative behavior by those who are trying to advance politically correct agendas? Because these agendas are not about tolerance; they're about power. And when power is confronted by the obvious (truth), a spiritual reaction occurs. Today we're seeing it played out in our country and around the world.

Truth is dangerous because it is contagious.

Jesus meets us in the middle of this insanity and says *He* wants to bring us peace. But to do so, He has to state the obvious by confronting us with the truth. Regardless of what we think about it or whether it contradicts some of the politically correct positions we are admonished to hold.

When He confronted those with differing opinions, and lifestyles, He did not shy away from saying what was obvious. Jesus did not tolerate sin. Neither did He condemn the person committing it. Instead, He showed them a better way—forgiveness.

Jesus' dual approach of love and forgiveness enabled people to receive what they were hearing, despite the sin they were entrenched in or the blindness that gripped them.

In our PC-crazy world, some continue to rail against the obvious, hoping that enough bluster will allow them to continue in their sin or in their lifestyles that Jesus challenged. In that case, Jesus will treat them like He confronted the money changers in the temple. They were scamming the people coming into the temple in need of an offering for their sacrifice.

What did Jesus do? He overturned the tables of the moneychangers and the benches of those selling doves and drove out all who were buying and selling there. He proclaimed with power that they had changed His house of prayer into a den of robbers

(Matthew 21:12–13). He wasn't being very tolerant then. And He's not today. But wasn't He also stating the obvious?

Jesus did not tolerate sin. Neither did he
condemn the person committing it. Instead He
showed them a better way—forgiveness.

He still chases out of us all the things we do and say that try to scam God of what's rightfully His in our lives. No amount of political will or negative press can erase the obvious facts of who Jesus is and what He claimed. He calls His followers to be North Stars for the world—people of peace, who exhibit true tolerance that engages all people and draws their hearts toward their Creator.

Jesus understood 2,000 years ago that stating the obvious would cost something. He called His followers to similar situations then, and today as well.

So, let the obvious be obvious, but let the intent in stating it be rooted in God's grace and peace.

Then maybe, just maybe, we'll stop screaming at each other long enough to listen. And learn.

Forgiveness allows us to
be released from ourselves.
Self-interest closes the gates
to this freedom.

9

The Upside-Down Kingdom

In Matthew 6, Jesus teaches His disciples a little prayer, which may be the most well-known prayer in Western civilization. We all know it as the "Our Father" or the Lord's Prayer. It starts off simply enough, "*Our Father, which art in heaven.*" Then it takes off from there to reveal something deeply profound.

Jesus had been talking about not praying with a lot of meaningless words like the religious people of His day liked to do. He made it clear that God already knew what we were going to pray about before we even uttered a word.

So, you might ask, why pray at all?

If you carefully look at what Jesus asked us to pray, this simple prayer was giving us a glimpse of the heavenly modus operandi for enjoying a quality of life here on earth. He meant to have us look outside of ourselves and beyond our circumstances to God's heavenly kingdom as the focal point for understanding earthly existence. The mystery, and the opportunity, is that we can experience now on earth the same kind of relationship that is experienced in heaven. They are one and the same.

Stop and think about that for a minute.

In effect, earth becomes the temporal training ground for the eternal.

Then why don't we see more of heaven on earth?

Because we want a god to conform to our image, rather than us conforming to His image. Which feeds right into the current politically correct mind-set that has supplanted the biblical world-view and "allows" us to set up a god of convenience according to our own standards.

Earth becomes the temporal
training ground for the eternal.

Even though this gives us a lot of latitude in the way we live our lives, it's also a poor substitute for achieving peace on earth and in our hearts. Jesus says that heaven is the frame of reference for earthly living. Political correctness reverses that order and says that man is the frame of reference. Something has to give.

He then adds several more similarities between the two kingdoms. And here's where it really gets interesting. One is forgiveness. The other is to eschew temptations that emanate from the evil one.

Forgiveness is a central theme because it's integral for entering and enjoying God's kingdom, so it's important to begin that lesson on earth.

We practice here and now for the real thing later on. We get a glimpse of it on earth and see it fully in action in heaven because only the forgiven and those who forgave will be there (Matthew 6:14–15). When put into practice, it has power to transform.

The most highly publicized example of that in our modern time is how Nelson Mandela exemplified the power of forgiveness to unite South Africa after he was released from prison and ascended to the highest political platform in the land.

Forgiveness allows us to be released from ourselves. Self-interest closes the gates to this freedom. It keeps us imprisoned and outside the kingdom and the joys that can be experienced on earth.

What impedes forgiveness like nothing else, says Jesus? Temptations. In fact, the concept is so important that He includes it in the "Our Father."

Jesus emphasizes resisting temptations because He knows it's the primary strategy of the evil one to sidetrack our focus from God and toward ourselves. Case in point is Jesus' experience in the wilderness. Satan threw a lot of temptations at Jesus…all designed to get Him to focus on Himself (Matthew 4:1–11).

Jesus wants us to know that there is a presence here on earth that seeks to destroy our view of the eternal with temptations. Temptations are clouds that block our view of all that is noble and good in the heavenly kingdom. They blur our vision of the eternal because they focus solely on the temporal to satisfy our natural desires.

Self-aggrandizement follows this kind of lifestyle. The more we focus on ourselves, the less we can focus on forgiveness. These two are tied together in some mystical way so that they reinforce the other.

That's why Jesus focuses so strongly on these two elements of how kingdom living can be achieved. There is no resisting of temptation without forgiveness, and no forgiveness without resisting the efforts of the evil one, who uses temptations as the cataracts of heavenly vision.

There is no resisting of temptation without forgiveness.

That's why political correctness is so devious in its approach. It's the devil all over again in the wilderness offering each of us opportunities to establish versions of our own kingdoms. When civilizations strip away the knowledge of a personal God involved in the affairs of man, they eventually implode. The temptation to be our own god begins to erode the opportunities of forgiveness that allow a nation or an individual to heal and be healed. It's the Tower of Babel syndrome for the twenty-first century—building a bigger platform to get closer to gods we create...ourselves.

You can always tell if a nation is following Jesus because at the center of their national persona is forgiveness and eschewing the temptation of self-interest. Conversely, nations that do not understand the power of forgiveness will always foster hate and mistrust or so focus on man as the center of the universe that it will give in to every temptation possible and begin to lose its compass for doing good.

If you want to see an example of that, just look at what happened during the French Revolution's Reign of Terror, or what's happened in Washington, or around the corner of your city. On a larger scale, we only need to look at countries that rule with hate and unforgiveness to see the end result of that way of life.

You can always tell if a nation is following Jesus because at the center of their national persona is forgiveness and eschewing the temptation of self-interest.

Political correctness would leave Jesus out of the marketplace as being too controversial. In doing so, we also leave out the very thing that would contribute to a civilized society when Jesus is at the core of the discussion. Where Jesus is, there's always a reminder that our earthly lives ought to be an expression of the heavenly kingdom... exemplified by thankfulness for what we have been given, forgiveness for others and ourselves, and the political will to stay away from the temptations that seek to destroy us.

Jesus came to show us what the heavenly kingdom could be like. He meets us along that road we walk through life and sets the stage for PC confrontation on earth because the two worlds (His kingdom and ours) are mutually exclusive.

Jesus asks us to turn our worlds upside down, so we can be right side up with God. And with each other.

So, ask yourself whether you are a microcosm of life in heaven right here on earth. If so, then thankfulness, forgiveness, and avoiding temptations that lead to destruction will be your prayer and the hallmarks of your life here on earth...as it is in heaven. Amen.

Is it "religious" to promote
loving your neighbor?

10

Guilt by Association

Several years ago, I read an article tucked away in the back pages of a newspaper that I thought captured the true spirit of the politically correct nonsense prevalent in our world today.

Liberty, Missouri, a suburb of Kansas City, had set up a community concert series to which its citizens were invited. I'm sure that many towns across our country have similar concert series free to the public. Well, one of the groups the town had invited to perform was Sidewalk Prophets, a band whose members are Christians. They've won a Dove Award, plus their songs appear regularly on the CCM charts.

But wait. The plot thickens. Seems like a local ACLU group representing the Kansas and Western Missouri Foundation region decided to issue a complaint to the city government citing the violation of the nebulous First Amendment prohibition against government endorsed "religion."

The actual letter sent by the ACLU states that their opposition is based on the fact the group is identified as a "contemporary Christian music group," and that their agreement allowed three-to-five minutes at each performance in support of American Bible Society's She's My Sister campaign on behalf of Congolese Women.[2]

Oh, the other problem was that Sidewalk Prophets asked attendees to bring a can of non-perishable food to benefit a food pantry run by a local church.

Nowhere in the complaint does it state that anyone from the ACLU attended the concert and heard what was being sung, or said from the stage, and it appears that the ACLU did not receive a complaint from anyone.

Let me be clear. The ACLU has been helpful in a number of cases where someone's civil rights were actually violated and have held people and organizations accountable for their actions. All good.

But it seems this is another case of the ACLU's angst against any possible Christian expression in the public square (if indeed it even happened in this case), which is clearly not the intent of the First Amendment's establishment of religion clause.

Of course, many Americans think that a separation of church and state clause is in the Constitution. It's not. Never was.

Many Americans think that a separation
of church and state clause is in the
Constitution. It's not. Never was.

From what I can tell by reading the ACLU's letter to the city, the problem seems to be that the ACLU decided to issue the complaint simply because the members of Sidewalk Prophets call themselves Christians and are defined as a contemporary Christian band. Much like how bands are defined by their style of music, whether it's rock, jazz, country, you name it. Contemporary Christian has become a style of music, and by the way, even a non-Christian can play a contemporary Christian song. Many songs are not specifically about "religion," but about issues and ideals that deal with spiritual themes or human rights situations that should be addressed from a moral perspective.

So, should Sidewalk Prophets not have been invited by the town of Liberty because the band members are Christians or because of how their music is defined? Would the ACLU have a problem with U2 playing in a community concert series if they were asked because Bono and The Edge claim to be Christians and often sing songs that deal with spiritual and political issues?

This is where the political correctness issue seems absurd. The problem wasn't that the ACLU received a complaint from anyone about Sidewalk Prophets' performance, or that they even have any information that the group used their platform to evangelize. No, they were there to sing their songs like any artist. Should they be penalized for their style of music?

Do their songs promote spiritual themes? Maybe. Is it "religious" to promote loving your neighbor by encouraging concert attendees to bring food for the local food pantry, even if it's run by a church? Or to promote the "She's My Sister" campaign to bring attention to the human rights violations committed against women and children in the Congo as a result of war? These were the things that the ACLU stated as being problematic in their letter to the governing body of Liberty.

Really?

Is it "religious" to promote loving your neighbor?

It seems the issue here is that Sidewalk Prophets is being singled out *because* of their faith…not because they did anything to step over that vague line of separation of church and state. The town of Liberty chose to ask this group to perform, not to evangelize on the town's dime, but because they were good enough to be asked. If the members of this group were avowed atheists, would the ACLU have objected as strongly?

Why even mention in the complaint the issue about the local

food pantry and trying to help women struggling to survive in the Congo? I doubt if the person receiving that food from the pantry cares that Sidewalk Prophets is a Christian band. On a sidenote, I wonder if the ACLU in that region ever gave food to that pantry.

Maybe the ACLU in this case might consider what's in their purview, instead of worrying about scenarios that never took place. Why all the effort? It comes down to fear. Fear that the town of Liberty had the audacity or ignorance or both to book a band with Christian roots to perform in a free community concert series.

It's these kinds of scenarios that drive me crazy. Jesus said our love for one another and compassion for the "least of these" would be the calling card of His true disciples.

Jesus said our love for one another and compassion for the "least of these" would be the calling card of His true disciples.

Prior to the modern welfare state we are saddled with in this country, the church was the prime facilitator of the care of indigent individuals, the establishment of orphanages, and of missions to feed the hungry and the poor. Christ-followers were constrained by their faith to be involved in the social ills of society, not out of duty but out of love first.

What our current political correctness fails to understand is that the very kinds of things everyone believes to be noble, regardless of where you are in the red- or blue-state spectrum, are the very things they attempt to stifle with their misplaced interpretations and biases.

Their mind-set reminds me of the Pharisees of old when they confronted Jesus for healing a paralytic on the Sabbath (Mark 2:1–12). These ancient forerunners of the ACLU were the PC police of their time. They were all up in arms that Jesus had performed such an act on the Sabbath when no one should be doing any work.

Instead of rejoicing that someone was healed, all the Pharisees could see was that one of their silly rules was broken.

In Liberty, Missouri, all the local ACLU group could see was that one of their silly lines of interpretations was crossed. Not that the local food pantry might be helped, or that a woman in the Congo who fears for her life might find hope and a safe haven.

> Instead of rejoicing that someone was healed, all the Pharisees could see was that one of their silly rules was broken.

This is what happens when you replace the spirit of the law with the letter of the law. You lose sight of the meaning of mercy, which is born from an act of love, and you replace it with a closed heart, which blinds you to compassion.

It would appear that the ACLU in this case, and from what I've read about other such cases, might be in danger of trying to take the speck out of the eyes of everyone before taking the plank or log out of their own.

Jesus calls people who do this *hypocrites*. "First take the plank out of your own eye," He says, "and then you will see clearly to remove the speck from your brother's eye" (Matthew 7:5).

That's why these kinds of cases advanced by the ACLU seem ridiculous to most of us. Having a plank in your eye prevents the ability to see things clearly. And if you can't see clearly, not only is your vision clouded but your heart, as well.

A cloudy heart is a serious disease. Jesus said He can help you overcome that…if you allow Him access to your heart. And that's one venue the ACLU will never have access to, even with all the assets of their legal machine.

When we lose our God-given moral compass, we lose our common sense. We cannot find within us that which can only be found outside of us.

11

The Common Sense of Counter Culture

In the introduction of this book, I defined political correctness as:

> The "chic" moral ideology of the day advocated and fleshed out in the public square by self-appointed gatekeepers of public opinion to the point where that definition becomes "fashionable."

To many of us, it seems we woke up one day, and the locks were changed to our dialogue with each other. We couldn't even get into the familiar places we once hung out intellectually. Instead of civil discussion on points of disagreement, heated arguments reigned, with screaming fests galore. Everyone now seems angry about something.

What happened?

Basically, someone sneaked in and changed our vocabularies without our permission. Long-standing definitions of *family, love, work, right,* and *wrong* were no longer acceptable. We had to redefine these terms and concepts to accommodate those who decided they didn't like the previous definitions. So, while many of us were busy getting on with our lives, the signposts to accepted cultural destinations were torn down and replaced with new names and new definitions.

> Someone sneaked in and changed our vocabularies without our permission.

Along with the new definitions came another rule. You could not disagree with the new rules because that was a sign of intolerance. Which, of course, makes no sense at all because disagreement and discourse are what an open society is about. When you begin to eliminate that free discourse, you invite a subtle brand of totalitarianism. A ruling elite surfaces, and the disparity between classes of people widens.

Does any of this look and sound familiar to current American cultural shifts? Is there any wonder our representatives in Washington, DC, seem like aliens from another planet? Just who are they representing?

So our culture began to move in a direction that many Americans disliked but did not have the power base or platform to disagree with loudly enough to be heard. We allowed the dissidents of faith and common sense to assume these platforms and impose themselves upon us.

As we used to say on the streets of Jersey, as I was growing up, to those who liked to give orders, "Who died and left you in charge?" No one ever accused us guys from North Jersey as being subtle. Today I feel like saying that same thing to all the PC police out there.

Political correctness is particularly disturbing to a Christ-follower and others who look for signposts beyond themselves for the way through life. Accepted cultural vocabulary has shifted away from the vocabulary of the kingdom of God to appease the new voices of political correctness that seek to dispel the notion of God from the marketplace.

Jesus commands his followers to not listen to the nonsense of political correctness because He was and is beyond politics and polemics. The PC police of Jesus' day were always trying out their "gotchas" on Him, only to hear Him say things that were so beyond their politically correct thinking that they couldn't even respond. He stymied them time and time again and revealed their hypocrisy to the point where they had to finally do something really radical, like partnering with the hated Romans to figure out a way to silence Him.

The PC police of Jesus' day were always trying out their "gotchas" on Him.

Jesus always stressed that His kingdom was not of this earth—that it had its own vocabulary and signposts that were erected by God. They were part of the fabric of the universe and not anything that man could merely decide to disregard. He underscored the fact that there's another way of looking at our world and how we respond to it that's different from what most people could grasp because His teachings are eternal and not subject to the whims of temporal interpretation. And that it requires a spiritual perspective only seen through eyes of faith that comes first and foremost by acknowledging Him.

And this is the issue we face today. Political correctness does not recognize the signposts that Jesus talked about. How could it? The current gatekeepers resemble the Pharisees whose minds and hearts were blinded to truth, and oblivious to anything beyond their own tightly held beliefs and experiences.

Our modern PC culture has taken great pains to have everyone believe that moral absolutes do not exist...which is absurd. Since the universe has physical absolutes that govern our relationship to the earth and the physical universe, why shouldn't moral absolutes also exist? Order demands absolutes so the universe can function.

Simply put, Jesus asks us to place His truth squarely in the center of human experience. His life was counter everything to the thinking of his day. And to our day. His life and His message are counterintuitive and countercultural. The entire Sermon on the Mount (Matthew chapters 5–7) was counterintuitive and countercultural. It espoused ideas, applications to life, and issues that were revolutionary and beyond the realm of man's reasoning at that time or *any* time.

Nothing has changed to this day. Jesus' message has remained the same through the centuries because He is beyond time. Jesus says He was before Abraham (John 8:58). John stated that Jesus was in the beginning with God, and all things were created through Him (John 1:1–3).

Scripture also claims that there's a moral fabric to the universe…sort of a universal moral compass that God has built into the DNA of each person (Romans chapters 1 and 2). And with that moral compass comes a common-sense approach and interaction with our world.

And this is why political correctness is dangerous. Not only does it promulgate intellectual dishonesty, it asks us to disregard the internal moral compass built into each of us by the Creator.

If I understand what Jesus is saying, when we lose our God-given moral compass, we lose our common sense.

Which takes us to where we are in America today. The further individuals and societies stray from a biblical morality, the more they decline in a common-sense approach to life. That's why there are so many examples of people exhibiting no common sense in our culture. We have replaced *common sense* with *nonsense*.

When we lose our God-given moral compass,
we lose our common sense.

To offset this growing lack of common sense, Jesus calls us to be counterculturalists in our response to society, much like He was during His time on earth. As society moves farther away from God's laws, Jesus asks us to remain centered by following that moral compass residing deeply within us. Not only does this keep us from being lost, it allows people who are desperate to find their true north. There is no true north under the relativism of political correctness.

Jesus also asks His followers to focus on how to relate to each other and to society in general, both of which are often counterintuitive. Jesus' examples of counterintuitive thinking are everywhere in the Bible. Take, for instance, "Whoever finds his life will lose it, and whoever loses his life for my sake will find it" (Matthew 10:39). Or, "So the last will be first, and the first will be last" (Matthew 20:16). These statements are counterintuitive because they defy the current moral direction of self-aggrandizement.

But Jesus also said these counterintuitive spiritual principles are discerned by having wisdom. They do not come just with knowledge or simply through human understanding. Psalm 111:10 says, "The fear of the LORD is the beginning of wisdom." That's where it starts.

Political correctness would have us look *inward* to discover truth. Jesus tells us to look *outward* to truth, which is embodied in Him. Truth and the wisdom of God does not exist within us; it only comes from God, who is outside of us.

Common sense is only common when our moral compasses are working. Strip away the moral compass, and you lose access to common sense. They work hand in hand. Because we've looked inwardly to determine our own moral compass, our society has paid a high price.

Political correctness would have us look *inward*
to discover truth. Jesus tells us to look *outward*
to truth, which is embodied in Him.

How? The more we look inwardly, the more fear we sense.

Stop there and ponder that poignant statement for a minute. Yes, I said the more we try to define our own truth, the more fear will become evident in our lives and in our corporate culture. Why?

Because we cannot answer the great questions of life by looking inside ourselves.

We cannot find within us that which can only be found outside of us.

Our society is now experiencing the results of their PC-induced experiments—a generation of confused individuals who are looking for truth inside themselves.

One blatantly obvious result is our violent society. Without a moral compass, we are adrift on the way to nowhere. That lack of true north breeds fear. Fear breeds anger and isolation. Did you ever stop to think why there is such an increase in violence in our schools?

The answer might simply be: Because we are afraid and have no hope. Fear breeds anger. And anger is what gets played out every day in our news.

Fear breeds anger and isolation.

The terrible increase in violent crimes in our schools against innocent children of all ages needs to be examined more closely and honestly by our society. We try to understand the sheer insanity of someone coming into a school with weapons to summarily kill our children. Of course, we can't, because acts like these are outside the realm of anything sensible.

So we seek reasons among the unreasonableness of it all. Let me suggest that it's not only because people have guns.

I do not own a gun. Never have. And I have no problem with those who do. But, for the life of me, I cannot understand the almost pathological irrationality of gun advocates who cannot agree to wait a few days for thorough background checks of individuals who purchase a gun. I mean, it took me three days to get my new refrigerator recently. And a week to get my new car. I can't wait a day to get my gun? I'm sorry, but that thinking eludes me.

But it's also irrational, and not very scientific, to blame all this on people having guns. People have always had guns. And they did not act like they do today. What's changed in the equation of society's makeup that now makes people use those weapons like never before on the most innocent and vulnerable of us?

When you conduct an experiment to see why something occurs in nature, you add elements into those environments until you find the cause. So the question we should be asking is, "What's new to our culture that may be the cause of our corporate angst that has turned people into serial killers at an alarming rate?"

Certainly it's not merely having a gun.

Or mental disease. We've always had those with mental issues among us.

So, what then?

> The question we should be asking is, "What's new to our culture that may be the cause of our corporate angst that has turned people into serial killers at an alarming rate?"

To ask that question and seek an honest answer, we'd have to have an intellectually honest discourse. A discourse that political correctness does not allow because we would have to introduce the notion of a moral law beyond the ones we make ourselves. And to agree to a moral law beyond us, we'd have to agree that there is a God.

Therein lies the problem. Can't do that because we'd offend all the atheists. And, truthfully, many of us like being our own god.

The answer may be that when we stripped away the moral compass, and lost our common sense, we became morally blind.

You can see the effect of this moral blindness everywhere. Reality (or "surreality," as I've called them) shows with people acting in ways that reflect no shame, no responsibility, no character. Blind politicians, bankers, civic leaders, me, and you. The blindness is pandemic.

Many of us like being our own god.

The good news is that Jesus healed the blind 2,000 years ago, and He can do so again today.

He asks us to receive our sight from Him and become the countercultural and counterintuitive agents to this world that will bring light and healing to those headed in the wrong direction without their true north.

When we begin to do that, and ask people to look outside of themselves to find their way (Jesus said He was *the* way in John 14:6), their fear will subside, as well. And anger will turn to calm. Then Jesus' voice can be heard above the nonsense saying, "Come to me, all you who are weary and burdened, and I will give you rest" (Matthew 11:28).

Jesus promises us a light yoke when we are harnessed to Him. The world promises us no yoke or harness and calls that *freedom*. Really? Freedom to be adrift on the way to nowhere? To be fearful? To constantly be searching for the more and more we are told will satisfy us, but it never does?

Is that really the *freedom* we're longing for?

I'd rather be harnessed to someone who loves me and promises me eternal life—starting now. That's called *commitment*.

The politically correct world promises me nothing like that.

Though it may be counterintuitive to some, Jesus asks us to be centered on Him and to let culture go its way without us.

I'll go with Jesus.

He promises me fullness of life…without being full of myself.

Talk about an easier way to live.

"YOUR GREAT NAME"

By Krissy Nordhoff & Michael Neale

Verse 1

Lost are saved; find their way; at the sound of your great name
All condemned; feel no shame, at the sound of your great name
Every fear; has no place; at the sound of your great name
The enemy; he has to leave; at the sound of your great name

Chorus

Jesus, Worthy is the Lamb that was slain for us, Son of God and Man
You are high and lifted up; and all the world will praise your great name

Verse 2

All the weak; find their strength; at the sound of your great name
Hungry souls; receive grace; at the sound of your great name
The fatherless; they find their rest; at the sound of your great name
Sick are healed; and the dead are raised; at the sound of your great name

Chorus

Jesus, Worthy is the Lamb that was slain for us, Son of God and Man
You are high and lifted up; and all the world will praise your great name

Bridge

Redeemer, my Healer, Lord Almighty
My Savior, Defender, You are my King

Chorus

Jesus, Worthy is the Lamb that was slain for us, Son of God and Man
You are high and lifted up; and all the world will praise your great name[3]

When you remove God from
the public square, ethical conduct
in that sphere diminishes.

12

Golden Rules
or Golden Calves?

D o unto others as you would have them do unto you." The
Golden Rule. Everyone can quote it.

Unfortunately, this long-revered maxim of civility seems to
have fallen on deaf ears of late. Looking out for the best interest
of the "others" has suffered a lot of bad press in recent years. The
money-making schemes by brand-name banks and investment
firms, personal investment counselors, and members of Congress
have not helped foster the Golden Rule very much.

So, what's all this have to do with political correctness?

Maybe nothing. But a closer look behind the curtain might
reveal an aspect of political correctness that has contributed to this
erosion of personal and corporate responsibility. Specifically, political correctness has no room for accountability to a personal God in
its worldview. And when you remove God from the public square,
ethical conduct in that sphere diminishes.

Biblical principles are thrown out the window, and God's laws
are ignored and even ridiculed. Self-sacrifice is soon replaced by

self-aggrandizement. And that spirit of self-aggrandizement begins to infect our culture corporately and personally.

Much like Moses' experience at Mt. Sinai (Exodus 32), people begin to look elsewhere for their significance and security when God's presence leaves the camp. Without leadership based on God's moral law, many of us will clamor for gods fashioned to fit our lifestyles and cravings. We worship the idols we've created to give us meaning to life.

Ironically, we've replaced the Golden Rule for golden calves.

> Without leadership based on God's moral law,
> many of us will clamor for gods fashioned to fit
> our lifestyles and cravings.

We lust for things that titillate and crave the things that make us comfortable and wealthy. Greed sets in, and we strip the land of all its worth. Today, the "lands" we plunder are our businesses, our institutions, and even our relationships. This "plunder-the-land" mentality burns bridges rather than builds them. Ultimately, with no moral constraint or concern for others, chaos ensues. And society crumbles under the weight of its sin.

When Moses came down the mountain, he saw the madness and lawlessness as a result of worshiping the golden calf. He had to literally throw the Word of God at the situation to stop the madness. We may need the same thing to happen today.

Our modern-day Aarons are supposed to be watching the camp, but they are swayed by the sultry voices of the craftsmen and artisans of delusion, whether they are found on Wall Street or Main Street. They know us well and play to our desire for gold-plated gods of money, security, celebrity, consumerism, power, and false religion. They have cleverly crafted these golden calves around which we revel and worship to our heart's content.

To the person worshiping the golden calf, the only future is today. Just as the Israelites did not want to wait any longer for Moses to come down the mountain with a word from God, neither do we. We're more interested in making our own gods and then putting words in their mouths to satisfy what we want to hear.

To the person worshiping the
golden calf, the only future is today.

So, look around you. Are you living out the Golden Rule, or dancing around the golden calf? God may not be politically correct in the public square. But, without Him, that square soon fills up with people dancing around idols of their own creation. King David has something to say about those types of people in the Psalms…that those who create God in their own image, made out of stone and wood, will ultimately be like them (Psalm 115). Hollow. Hard. Unbending.

Ultimately, we wind up worshiping ourselves. That's a scary thought. I don't know about you, but I'd make a terrible idol.

It's a hard thing
to handle absolute truth.

13

Security in
an Insecure World

I had the real privilege to interview Corrie ten Boom some years ago. To those unfamiliar with her, the amazing story of how she and her family hid Jews from the Nazis and were betrayed and sent to concentration camps was told in the inspirational book and movie *The Hiding Place*.

When I met her, she was in her eighties. She looked like my diminutive Italian grandmother, so I felt right at home with this unlikely hero. As we talked, she shared a number of stories from those days of horror and how her faith sustained her. One thing she said has stuck with me for 40 years now. It was simply this: "Don't hold onto anything so tightly that Jesus can't take it from you."

It was one of those moments permanently etched in the timeline of my life. And a fascinating moment for a young journalist to take in some spiritual wisdom from someone who had all the right to be angry with God...and bitter at life. But only grace and joy exuded from her spirit.

Corrie helped me better understand what security is really all about. Truth is, embracing a counterculture faith stands in stark contrast to the current politically correct understanding of what constitutes security.

Security is a major concern of the American lifestyle, as it is for all countries and people worldwide. Or, rather, insecurity is. Terrorism, failing financial institutions and failing relationships, and dysfunctional governance on the local, state, and national levels all contribute to the growing sense of insecurity in our world.

> "Don't hold onto anything so tightly
> that Jesus can't take it from you."
> —Corrie ten Boom

Still, everyone is looking for security, but it's elusive to most. When that happens, people will look anywhere, and do anything, to attain it.

Paradoxically, Jesus suggested that we best realize security when we stop our pursuit of being in control and trust Him. That's what Corrie ten Boom was alluding to in her comment.

Understanding that perspective, Jesus says, should put us at rest. He's telling us that security is best understood as a trust relationship and not a theological concept. Understanding theology only brings us to the point of belief. Knowing Jesus takes us over that line of belief to the crux of the issue, which is not whether we can lose security, but rather, can God lose control of His universe. Corrie ten Boom learned the distinction between the two in the crucible of a concentration camp.

But, in a politically correct world that demands the removal of the presence of God from the marketplace of ideas, we are left with interpreting security on our own terms. We work hard at trying to define the concept or attain it. Yet, the harder we try to achieve security, the more fear builds up in our lives.

Fear is the "natural resource" of an insecure world. Or of an insecure person who then lives an uncertain life.

Fear is played out daily in our culture, expressed in one of two ways—either by anger or control. Those are the two sides of the same coin.

Everyone is looking for security, but it's elusive to most. When that happens, people will look anywhere, and do anything, to attain it.

The anger side of that coin is evidenced by the front page headlines screaming at us about the most recent road rage display, bullying incident, or senseless random act of violence.

The control side of the coin is much more subtle. But it plays itself out in the culture at large and even in the church. Fear that leads to control allows unscrupulous people (say, political and church leaders) to build power bases (constituents and congregations) to exercise control over others to achieve a shadowy form of security.

Jesus understood what happens when people lose sight of who's in control of the world, and who their security truly is. He continually points to Himself as the One who can bring peace to the heart that yearns to be secure (John 14:27).

The more society removes the presence of a personal God, the more it reflects the results of that action—fear leading to anger or control. Ultimately, we fear the very thing that would remove our fear. Fear builds fences in a land of no boundaries…imaginary lines over which we dare not cross. Another disastrous result of politically correct thinking.

Ultimately, if God is love, and we remove God from the equation, we will remove love from all aspects of life. What will we replace it with? All kinds of distractions and fake love to satisfy that innate, hardwired need for God's love that reminds us of who is in control and where our security really lies.

Take a look at Matthew 6 sometime. The entire chapter is a call to counterculture faith. Our world tells us to hold on to our lives and hoard our possessions. Jesus tells us to let go of ourselves and give away all we own to follow Him. His perspective on security is for us to stand guard over nothing, to have possessions of no value, vaults with no money. After all, if there's nothing to take, there's nothing to watch.

That time with ten Boom taught me that what is out of my control falls into the realm of Romans 8:32: "He who did not spare his own Son, but gave him up for us all—how will he not also, along with him, graciously give us all things?" It would be helpful to grapple with and begin to learn and act on the significance of that passage so that when we find ourselves holding on to things tightly, we have the freedom to let go.

> If there's nothing to take,
> there's nothing to watch.

The American mind-set would demand that we have the right to all these things and to hold on to them. Ironic how we want to hold on to the things that can't be controlled and reject the things that keep the universe, and us, under control, such as the laws of God.

Our all-too-human tendency is to hold on tightly and not let go of the things we value too much.

Sort of reminds me of how monkeys are trapped. The monkey easily fits its hand into the hollowed end of a gourd with food in it. But when he makes a fist to pull out the food, the monkey can't get the food or his fist out. You'd think the monkey would just let go of the food and slip out his hand. No! Instead he continues to hold onto the food, thereby preventing his escape. Ultimately, he traps himself.

Before we think the monkey stupid, we should look at the way we attempt to hold onto things that will eventually ensnare us.

God's way out of the traps set by life's circumstances is to give up control. Only after we let go can God use us. He will not hold on to us if we prefer to hold on to something else.

Our all-too-human tendency
is to hold on tightly and not let go of
the things we value too much.

I've learned, along life's journey, that whatever I cannot control, I must release. If I do so, that action frees me to carry on my life so that He's in control. That's all God ever wants.

So, if you're looking for security, read what Jesus had to say. He asks us to not listen to the voices in culture that suggest we find security by grabbing for all we can get.

Remember the words of Corrie ten Boom: "Don't hold on to anything so tightly that Jesus can't take it from you."

He may have need of it someday.

If we draw a line in the sand,
our love ought to be more evident
to the world than our doctrine.

14

The Shape of Sin

I t all started in the garden. Sin, that is.

Yes, that simple, old-fashioned way of looking at the world and why humankind acts the way it does. Actually, the word *sin* is derived from an old English term that was used to mark the distance from the center of the bull's-eye in archery tournaments. It's basically missing the mark.

A lot of us miss the mark on a number of things in life. Some of it may be sin—that predisposition in our human nature to do something outside of the laws of God. Or you can call it "going our own way." However you like to define it.

When we look back to the garden account, how man reacted when he first "sinned" is telling. As told from Genesis, chapter 3, Eve eats a fruit from the tree of the Knowledge of Good and Evil, and with a little encouragement from the serpent, the first act of rebellion enters the human race.

What's interesting to me is that Adam and Eve first became aware of their nakedness only *after* they ate the fruit (verse 7). What happened? Could it be that some knowledge was revealed to them that had not been known previously?

Basically, self-awareness was now introduced into the world.

Self-awareness allows us to acknowledge ourselves, which is healthy, of course. Until self-awareness leads to self-importance. Which leads to self-reliance. Which leads us away from the Creator.

Adam and Eve knew something was different. So they did the only thing they could think of to do. They gathered what they could find—fig leaves—and managed to sew them together in an attempt to cover their nakedness.

But their new self-awareness also revealed to them something new, as well.

Their sin.

Adam and Eve first became aware of their nakedness only *after* they ate the fruit.

Scripture says that God found them hiding and made their first clothes as a way of covering them (verse 21). That was quite symbolic. I really believe that God was covering their shame, which was lying to Him, and had nothing to do with them being naked.

We've been covering up our shame ever since.

God first covered man with the skins of animals after the first sin and then ultimately covered their sin by the person of Jesus. And here is where we find the interesting disconnect of political correctness and what Jesus taught.

Whether one actually believes in the garden account and that a real Adam and Eve walked the earth is really not the issue. PC thought would question biblical authority and historicity and the notion of absolute truth. It would also say that there really is no sin because, to acknowledge sin, you have to acknowledge a moral code that gives a definition of right or wrong and meaning to an action or thought. There has to be a "bull's-eye" that we miss.

However, PC thought says there really is no bull's-eye because there is no one absolute moral code. Society becomes the progenitor of its own moral code to know where the line is between right and wrong.

But then whose moral code or morality do we use as the measure throughout history? That of communist China, the former apartheid regime of South Africa, openly racist America of just a few years ago, or socialist Europe?

Society becomes the progenitor
of its own moral code to know where
the line is between right and wrong.

A moral code is rules driven. It has no power or life in and of itself to prevent someone from sinning. It merely provides a good mirror to reflect in and observe right and wrong.

So, along comes Jesus and provides a different twist on the Adam and Eve story and sin. Jesus loved people but never tolerated their sin. There was always a distinction. The woman caught in adultery is the classic example (John 8:1–11).

Fast forward to our current culture. Today, Jesus still speaks out against sin, while political correctness defends it. Or denies its very existence.

We now tolerate both the sin and the sinner, and go even one step further. We celebrate, and even lionize, those individuals (along with their actions and attitudes) whose celebrity is their sin. It becomes their entrée to a politically correct world. We give them reality television shows and hold them up as celebrities for missing the mark of God's love for them.

Interestingly, the one thing I always ask myself when I see someone or a group acting in such a fundamentally coarse and embarrassing way is, "Where is their shame?"

Then I realize a most obvious response—while Adam and Eve hid from God because of their shame, today we've come full circle as a society that celebrates shame above virtue. The more we reject

God's coverings, the further we leave behind God's grace and the more shameful we will become. And the more we will want to hide from God.

While Adam and Eve hid from God because of their shame, today we've come full circle as a society that celebrates shame above virtue.

Our society is paying the price for hiding from God. Though we will not admit it, we try to cover ourselves up with drugs, dishonest relationships, or even "success." You name it. But, in the end, God peeks through the bushes to look at our fig-leaf coverings and says, "Did you think you could hide from Me?"

John 8:1–11 tells the story of the woman caught in the act of adultery. When she was deposited in front of Jesus by her accusers, did he lambaste her for her sins? No, he simply started writing on the ground with his finger and made a statement that drove away her accusers, one by one: "If any one of you is without sin, let him be the first to throw a stone at her" (verse 7).

After her accusers melted away, Jesus talked with the woman and told her, "Go now, and leave your life of sin" (verse 11).

A simple but powerful statement that transformed her life.

When those in the church say similar things, though, in what spirit do we say them? With a judging spirit? Or with the loving, forgiving, yet not-putting-up-with-the-sin spirit that Jesus exhibited toward the woman caught in adultery?

The world must sense that the spirit in which that phrase is spoken overrides the church's often unbending measuring stick of biblical self-righteousness.

In other words, our lines in the sand must speak quietly for themselves so that Christ's love is always more evident to the world than His doctrine.

So, what shape is your sin in? Are you embarrassed by it? Do you need a little shaping up? Or, do you like to flaunt your sin and elevate your shame to where people applaud you for it?

Our lines in the sand must speak quietly for themselves so that Christ's love is always more evident to the world than His doctrine.

Christ came to once again be the covering from God for our rebellion, our sin. We can accept that and find peace. Or we can hide from Him and spend our time and energy going from one bush to another in our own fig-leaf clothing, hoping that God will not see us.

It's time to come out from hiding…and to enjoy the peace Jesus promises. "Peace I leave with you, my peace I give you." He says, "I do not give to you as the world gives, Do not let your hearts be troubled and do not be afraid" (John 14:27).

The sacred cow stands as a symbol of what the herd has been through and survived. As a result, the sacred cow becomes untouchable. Even if starvation comes to the camp, people would rather die than kill the sacred cow.

15

Steak from the Sacred Cow

I used to love Westerns. When I was a kid, I watched faithfully all the weekly Westerns on television that came from the Warner Brothers studio. I also loved Western movies. Anything with John Wayne in particular. They were always full of action and adventure.

If it was a Western, you could probably count on seeing cattle in the movie. And if there were cattle, there would probably be a stampede at some point. Something would spook those cows, possibly rustlers, howling coyotes, a gunshot, thunder and lightning... you name it. Wouldn't take much to get those cows running toward nowhere.

Inevitably, someone would get caught in the middle of that stampede and lose his life. Wagons would be toppled; some of the cows might be killed. It was a mess.

Funny how all the cows would be down for the night, resting peacefully, and then all of a sudden, from nowhere the stampede would begin. It only took a few cows to get them all going. Then the whole herd would follow. Thousands of cows running wildly in all directions! Imagine, it took only a few to start all that damage.

Can you picture one cow turning to another and asking, "Where are you going in such a rush?"

"I don't know," replies the second cow. "I'm just following the guy up there. Must be important. Otherwise, why would we be running so fast?"

It only took a few cows to get them all going.
Then the whole herd would follow.

Well, I don't get to see too many of those old movies anymore. But life in the church can easily resemble a Western sometimes.

There are professional stampeders who will bolt when frightened and get others to follow them blindly. They create a fuss that affects everyone around them. Unfortunately, the church also can have its own politically correct agenda, so it's only fair to look inward on this one.

Let's identify three of these types of stampeders.

One is the sacred cow. Now, the sacred cow is a strange animal. It's been around forever and has the respect of the herd for a number of reasons. He's always known exactly the right trail to follow to find food and water for the other cows, so many of the cows trust him. That's reassuring.

The sacred cow also stands as a symbol of what the herd has been through and survived. As a result, the sacred cow has become more than just another animal. He becomes untouchable. Even if there's starvation in the camp, people would rather die than kill the sacred cow.

Because of his track record, a lot of other cows revere the grass where he grazes. Any cow that suggests grazing elsewhere gets ignored, or even condemned.

"We've always grazed here," they say. "This has always been the best grass for grazing. How can it be any better somewhere else?"

Even if there's starvation in the camp, people
would rather die than kill the sacred cow.

Regrettably, the sacred cow knows only one way. Although he's been right for a long time, lately he hasn't followed the weather patterns to know that the watering hole dried up. He simply keeps going back, expecting the water to be there. Neither he nor the rest of the herd will discover this until it's too late. The consequences could be tragic.

In a sense, the sacred cow stampedes the herd into believing him. It may not be a full-out run, but it's just as dangerous because it's not readily apparent. Regardless, it still could be deadly to a lot of cows, mostly the weak ones or the newborns.

Not keeping up with what's happening around him often leads to a sad ending for the sacred cow. What's sadder is that his lack of foresight can endanger the other cows in the herd. Some may even die. The road taken by the sacred cow can often be strewn with carcasses of dead cows.

Another stampeder is the bull-headed cow. He acts more like a bull than a cow. He swaggers like a bull and throws his weight around like a bull, but he's only a cow. He doesn't like to follow anyone. He'll often wander off because he'd rather blaze a trail of his own. Yet, time after time, the cowboy brings the bull-headed cow back to the herd, regardless of how many times he strays.

Regrettably, the bull-headed cow often leads other cows along on his meanderings. Many times, the bull-headed cow and his pals get lost, disrupting the schedule of the drive. On their selfish pursuits, one day this cow will get himself and his friends in trouble. He'll separate from the rest of the herd and run into a pack of hungry wolves that will attack when he's weakest and alone. No cowboy will be around to save him then. But that's what he gets for being so bull-headed.

> The bull-headed cow doesn't like to
> follow anyone. He'll often wander off
> because he'd rather blaze a trail of his own.

Then, there's the really, really smart cow. This cow knows more than the cowboy and will challenge the cowboy's authority. And because of the force of personality, other cows will follow this smart cow. This is another kind of stampede that often will split the herd. The smart cow knows nothing about nurturing the other cows. Just himself.

Ironically, all three types of cow are part of the same drive and herd. The sacred cow lives in the past, and as a result, forfeits the future. The bull-headed cow doesn't care about the past or the future, and lives for the present. And the smart cow's focus is always on itself. They are all so different, yet similar.

> The really, really smart cow…knows more
> than the cowboy and will challenge
> the cowboy's authority.

Jesus warned us about following other cows, rather than the cowboy. And He had stern words for those cows in the herd that lead other cows astray. In Matthew 18:6, Jesus says that it would be better for someone to have a large millstone hung around his neck and be thrown into the sea than to cause one of His children to go astray. That's pretty powerful.

Jesus also says in Matthew 11:30 that when we take His yoke upon us, it's easy and light. Cows often will get these heavy yokes put on them to enable them to do heavy work. Not so with Jesus' yoke. He promises: "Come to me, all you who are weary and burdened, and I will give you rest. Take my yoke upon you and learn from me, for I am gentle and humble in heart, and you will find rest for your souls" (Matthew 11:28–29).

So, you might want to look at the herd you're hanging with. Don't let the sacred cow or the bull-headed cow or the smart cow lead you apart from Jesus to follow them. They're not interested in getting you to the watering hole. Rather, they're interested in doing their own thing, which is usually not in your own best interest!

Remember, there may be wolves out there, waiting for just the right time to pounce on an unsuspecting cow.

Anyone for steak dinner?

There is an undeniable link between the God of the universe and the universe itself, just as an artist has a spiritual connection with his art and often creates art that reflects what's deep down in his soul.

16

God, Gardens, and Green Zones

I love spring—the time of year when I come out of winter hibernation and colors come alive once again all around me. What a reminder that life has beauty if we only take the time to see it. Smell it. Walk in it.

This past spring also prompted me to think about something I never had considered, which came up during a conversation with friends.

We were talking about health, nutrition, and overall spiritual health. Somehow the topic turned to how much I always enjoyed working in a garden…part of my built-in DNA, I believe, stemming from my Italian heritage and the many hours I spent working in the rather large garden we had in our yard at home. My grandfather, uncle, father, brother, and I would tend it.

When my grandfather was alive, he would prepare the entire garden—almost 10,000 square feet—by hand with a pitchfork. Of course, he was used to hard work because that's all he ever knew. It seemed that extreme perspiration was part of being Italian. Which may explain why I became a journalist.

After my grandfather passed away, my father and uncle decided to get close to the twentieth century and get a rototiller to do all that work. We were basically self-sufficient in the summer as we grew every fruit and vegetable imaginable.

I have never felt more content and at peace than sitting in the dirt on a sunny summer day planting tomatoes, cucumbers, squash, and other vegetables in my garden.

Being one with nature is very much a biblical principle, for several reasons.

The psalmist declares that the heavens reveal the glory of the Lord (Psalm 19:1). Paul, in Romans, reminds us that God's handiwork is revealed in nature and in the heavens (Romans 1:20). Jesus alludes to God's care and presence in His creation when He asks us to trust and not worry about today, for He clothes the flowers of the field and provides food for the birds (Matthew 6:25–34).

Yes, there is an undeniable link between the God of the universe and the universe itself, just as an artist has a spiritual connection with his art and often creates the art that reflects what's deep down in his soul.

If we sit and listen to nature and observe, it is God's silent language to us that reveals much about His character. We see order, beauty, purpose, and breathtaking majesty, as well as force and power and even destruction.

There is an undeniable link between the God
of the universe and the universe itself.

So, it seems to be evident that because nature reveals and speaks to us of God, the less of nature and the natural world, the less to speak of God's existence. As such, the Christian should be the most ardent of all conservationists. After all, to remove the creation is to remove something that God created to bear witness of Himself.

So, does it make sense as well that when we surround ourselves with less of God's creation (clean air, trees, grass, lakes and rivers, and creatures) we remove an aspect of God's presence from our lives?

I've come to believe that this is one of the prime reasons we have such chaos in cities, crime is more prevalent, there is less peace, and liberal thinking is dominant. I use *liberal* in this case not in the classic meaning of "generous" but in the new sense of going against biblical patterns of thought and principles to embrace an ideology of godlessness.

Yes, you heard me. Our major cities tend to skew liberal because a vestige of God's presence has been removed from the environment, thereby making it harder to find God.

I admit, I'm no social scientist, and this line of reasoning may be way off in left field somewhere. But I have come to believe that it may not be so much that cities have more people, and the percentages of people necessarily would create more opportunity for crime and godlessness.

> Our major cities tend to skew liberal
> because a vestige of God's presence
> has been removed from the environment,
> thereby making it harder to find God.

Instead, it may be that the environment has been so stripped of God's presence that we have lost sight of Him and His place in our lives. And if we strip away the things of nature that by design communicate a sense of order, tranquility, and transcendence, then society will gravitate toward the antithesis of those things—disorder, stress, and focus on self, which breeds selfishness. Without a God to embrace, we create our own gods to fill that vacuum in our souls for which we've been hardwired.

I really believe the trend toward urban gardening is fueled by an innate drive for people to experience the peace of God in the midst of urban culture that sucks life from us and from our spirits.

The movement in the eighteenth and nineteenth centuries to build parks in the middle of urban environments—Central Park in New York being the most dominant—was a direct correlation to provide people with a glimpse of God, a retreat opportunity for citizens to refuel and relax. And the great architects of these parks and gardens, for the most part, were biblicists.

Without a God to embrace, we create
our own gods to fill that vacuum in our souls
for which we've been hardwired.

So, if you're feeling far from God, take a trip to the country. Be still.

Better yet, put on some old clothes and go sit in the dirt and plant some tomatoes. Listen to the voice of God in the wind as it whips through the trees. Feel His presence in the warmth of the sun.

Pray. Sing a worship song.

I bet you'll feel a lot better at the end of the day.

"A Glimpse of You"
By Joe Battaglia

Lord, I thank You for Your creation
and how it mirrors Your image.
When we retreat to Your kingdom,
it's not merely to view animals, lakes, and trees,
but to catch a glimpse of You as You speak to us.

Father, we see You in the dragonfly as it darts to and fro,
and in the ant as it appears to be in a state
similar to the last shopping day before Christmas.
We see You in the spider as it clumsily waddles along,
seemingly in all four directions at once.

The dragonfly, the ant, and the spider are all Your creations
and used by You, no matter how unseemly
or useless they appear.
When will we learn from them to appreciate who we are?
I wonder if an ant ever wanted to be a dragonfly?

Father, we see You in the beautiful, clear lake
that invites us to swim in its clear, cool waters.
And when we leave the lake,
as when we leave Your presence,
we are refreshed.

The lake, too, bears Your image.
Father, we see You in the mighty trees,
as they point upward toward You.
When You blow on them during a storm,
they know their place in Your kingdom
and bow quietly before You in an attitude of respect for Your power.

When will we learn from the tree, tall and strong and proud,
yet humble enough to bow before its Creator,
when called upon, and not fight back.
Father, when will we learn the secrets of Your creation?
When will our nature match Yours?

Our culture needs
more than just preserving.
It needs replenishing.

17

Parable of the Fertilizer

When I was a kid, I lived with my parents, brother, and paternal grandparents in a small North Jersey town not far from New York City. Being very Italian, we had a very large garden. As a result, every spring a large amount of fertilizer was delivered to help us prepare the soil for planting. It wasn't the kind you get today at Home Depot in bags. No, this fertilizer came in truckloads from the local chicken farm. Chicken droppings were really good as a fertilizer. It had quite an aroma, as you could imagine, but it was effective. No doubt, fertilizer has its place and a significant purpose.

Okay, now hold that thought while I introduce another one.

In Matthew 5:13–16, Jesus describes His followers as salt and light. He tells them plainly, so there can be no misunderstanding: "You are the salt of the earth. But if the salt loses its saltiness, how can it be made salty again? It is no longer good for anything, except to be thrown out and trampled by men. You are the light of the world. A city on a hill cannot be hidden. Neither do people light a lamp and put it under a bowl. Instead they put it on its stand, and it gives light to everyone in the house. In the same way, let your light shine before men, that they may see your good deeds and praise your Father in heaven."

What are the distinguishing characteristics of those who would be called His disciples? They would be like salt, to flavor and act as a preservative to society. And they would be like light, to illumine the beauty and presence of God in this world and to dispel the darkness that would blind men to all that is good in the world.

Ultimately, all this salting and lighting would point people to God, and not to us. Unfortunately, at times, and often in our culture, evangelicals have exhibited more traits of the chicken fertilizer from my childhood than those of salt and light!

Fertilizer is to be spread evenly over the land to enrich and nourish the environment so that things can grow and be fruitful. Fertilizer is useful, even necessary at times, to replenish the land with nutrients so it can be productive. Without fertilizer, the land may not be able to sustain the growth of good plants. Weeds don't have that problem as they seem to grow anywhere and everywhere without the aid of fertilizer. They're prolific and can choke the growth of the good plants. Fertilizer can help control the weeds by creating the right climate for good plants to grow so the weeds don't take over the land. All good.

Fertilizer is useful,
even necessary at times,
to replenish the land with nutrients
so it can be productive.

Now, take that same fertilizer and stockpile it somewhere. We used to do that before we used it. We knew it was there; we couldn't miss it. After all, if fertilizer is stockpiled too long without being spread throughout the land and used as the enriching agent it's meant to be, it begins to fester, smell, and even attract flies. Instead of contributing to the overall productivity of the soil, it becomes useless. Things grow in the fertilizer, but not the plants you intended to grow. And, if the fertilizer is not spread out, nothing grows anywhere else. Outside of that stockpiled area, the plants start to die and weeds take over.

It dawned on me that sometimes Christ-followers resemble fertilizer. They are meant to be spread throughout the land as an enriching agent, not to remain in one area. They are to provide a valuable element of God's presence to bring life to barren lives and aid in the growth of those who can't make it alone. A Christian is more than salt and light in the world because our culture needs more than just *preserving*. It needs *replenishing*.

That's the job of fertilizer. And that's our unique calling. Ideally, we should be known by the way we enrich the world by our presence.

Our culture needs more than just *preserving*.
It needs *replenishing*.

On the other hand, if Christians stockpile themselves in one area without being the enriching agents they were meant to be, they begin to fester, even smell, if you know what I mean. It's not a pleasant sight or odor when that happens. And if you happen to be downwind of them...

So, I'm taking liberty with what Jesus said and adding another trait of the Christ-follower's persona. He is to be like fertilizer, along with salt and light.

Are you preserving the land? Or do you remain in the salt-shaker and clump together with the rest of the salt? You know what happens then. The longer it stays in that shaker, the harder it is to shake loose, right? Is your light pleasant to be around? Or is it blinding? Just what are you illuminating anyway?

And, finally, are you acting like fertilizer? Spreading out to enrich our land—or stockpiling yourself with other believers?

By the way, what's that I smell? Just thought I'd ask.

The life of limited options
is a life of freedom.

18

The Freedom
in Limitations

Guys like to fix things. I'm no exception.

We are hardwired to make things right. If there's a problem, whether in our company or in our relationships, we want to fix it. We like to check off things on our "to do" lists, then move on to the next thing to conquer. There's a little Don Quixote in all of us—dreaming the impossible dreams and fighting the unbeatable foes. But sometimes we cannot find solutions, despite how hard we fight for them.

My wife has multiple sclerosis (MS). The good news is that we found an incredible doctor who halted its progression without drugs or anything invasive. He's brilliant. The bad news is that my wife was in a wheelchair prior to finding this doctor, and she still is not able to stand and walk.

Try as I might, I may not be able to fix my wife's symptoms of MS. So, life can be hard as a caregiver. I have to give up some things I enjoy doing. Change my life, basically. Sublimate my needs for another's.

Well-meaning guys will come up to me and say something like, "I don't know how you do it." I assume they mean how I take care of my wife, deny myself some of life's assumed pleasures, and not walk around looking dejected and robbed of joy. Well-meaning comments, but devoid of context.

I used to feel bad, until I had a change of perspective. You see, it dawned on me that the limitations imposed on me as a result of my wife's MS have actually enhanced my understanding of freedom. My options have been limited in what I can do, where I can go, how long I can stay away on business trips, etc. I have fewer choices because my situation robs me of choice.

In a convoluted sort of way, the less I have to choose from, the more freedom I find in that limitation.

Look at it from another perspective. Everyone knows about gravity. It's the force that keeps us on planet earth. Otherwise, we'd float away into space. Now, what you may not realize is that the mass of the earth is what creates gravity. Simple physics. The more mass, the more pull. The more pull and attraction, the harder it is to break free.

Our culture encourages us to accumulate things, to have options, to focus on ourselves. The problem is that the more things we accumulate, the more mass we create. And the more mass, the more pull. Soon we cannot pull ourselves away from the things we've accumulated because they have such a hold on us. They control us; we do not control them. We attempt to break free, but the pull is too strong.

The more mass, the more pull. The more pull and attraction, the harder it is to break free.

The only thing that can free us is an opposite force sufficiently powerful to overcome the gravity of our situation. We need help beyond ourselves.

That's why limitation is so powerful. It not only helps us lessen the mass that keeps holding us down, but it also enables us to see that we are in need of help…that opposing force.

Here's an example. Since 9-11, national and personal security has become the major issue facing our nation. We want to be secure from terrorism. From government intrusion. From compromised borders. From identity theft. And the list goes on.

An insanity of insecurity has overtaken us. Our former rock-like symbols of security have become pebbles of annoyance in our shoes. *In God We Trust* may still be inscribed on our currency, but it's no longer on our hearts. To many, apart from a deadbolt lock on our door and a million dollars in the bank (or under your mattress if you don't trust banks), security is virtually nonexistent.

In God We Trust may still be inscribed on our
currency, but it's no longer on our hearts.

Still, everyone looks for security, but it remains elusive to most. It's become harder to find because we no longer look for it where it can be found. As our world nosedives out of control, insecurity increases. And American culture currently throws fuel on the fire of insecurity instead of putting it out.

The by-product of insecurity and loss of control is fear.

Insecurity is not caused by the presence of fear, but rather by the absence of control.

Paradoxically, the Bible suggests that security is best realized when we relinquish the pursuit of being in control and surrender to God. Jesus describes the issue of control in Matthew 6, pointing to God's care and concern for one of the smallest of His creatures, the sparrow (verse 26). Understanding that perspective, Jesus says, should give us confidence and rest. He asks us to view life through another set of eyes.

Security is best realized when we relinquish the
pursuit of being in control and surrender to God.

Then Jesus asks us to do something very un-American. He asks us to surrender. That word is not popular in any language. But with the historical American mind-set of independence, and iconic and legendary battles such as Bunker Hill, The Alamo, etc., etched in our corporate pride, *surrender* is definitely not popular in our vocabulary.

But it was in Jesus' vocabulary. His surrender, though, was in a form no one quite understood. In fact, it's still hard to come to grips with it. Jesus is God, yet He surrendered His will to that of the Father's. Jesus says in John 6:38, "For I have come down from heaven not to do my will but to do the will of him who sent me."

Christ's agenda was to merely do the will of the Father. That provided him all the security He needed.

It should do likewise for us. We like our independence. We think we have rights. I'd like my independence from my wife's MS. But Jesus comes into that thinking and shatters it entirely. He says we have no rights.

This issue of surrender as a way to feel secure seems totally incomprehensible to us as human beings. If we could only get to the point where we don't understand surrender as a *loss of control,* but *a relinquishing of the lack of control.* We are to surrender what we actually do not own—ourselves.

That's what Jesus was trying to say to any who listened: "You are living under the illusion of control." Ultimately He was saying, "I'm the one and only one who can offer you salvation and freedom." Frankly, I'll take my chances with God in control.

I have found that the life of limited options is a life of freedom. Free from the gravitational pull of things…free to see more clearly the life that God has given to us and free to produce more joy because we focus less on ourselves and more on others. We have less to divert our attention away from the things that matter.

The life of limited options is a life of freedom.

It's not enough to just understand theology. That only takes us to the point of belief. But trusting in God makes it a reality.

So, looking for real freedom and security? It may be in living the life of limited options. Because when you surrender, you no longer have the need to control anything. There's nothing left for you to control.

How freeing is that!

There is no litmus test to gain access to the foot of the cross, which is the greatest level playing field of all time.

19

Power to
the People

During the late 1960s and early 70s, I was a student at Boston University. It was during the height of all the student unrest on college campuses nationwide. BU was no different. In fact, it was called "The Berkeley of the East" due to the large amount of "radical" activity at that time on the campus.

We had Students for a Democratic Society (SDS), Weathermen (The Weather Underground), Hari Krishna, openly avowed communists, and a host of other groups that contributed to this amazingly electric atmosphere on the campus. The aroma of marijuana was everywhere...in the student union, study halls, and in Fenway Park. The joke I always told my friends back home was that I never smoked, but most definitely inhaled. Unless you were able to hold your breath all day, it would be impossible not to. Boring it was not.

Among the many "colorful" words and new terms that were prevalent back then, one phrase in particular became an anthem of sorts to many involved in the antigovernment protest movement during those late 1960s. It was "Power to the People," which reflected the naïve thinking that the "people"—the everyday masses—should take back power from the political parties and ruling elite in order to form a more egalitarian society.

The only problem was that once someone got power they soon learned how hard it was to handle. Power has a habit of consuming those who seek it, and it ultimately will turn on them like Frankenstein's monster, totally out of control.

Today, political correctness also says that it wants to give power to the people. But there's a catch. Political correctness desires to exercise control over the process. But unlike the 60s, it wants to control cultural thought instead of political power in order to further its agenda.

In the midst of this new "cultural thought" revolution, it's always good to remind ourselves of the kind of power and control that Jesus identified as characteristics of those who belong to Him. They contradict much of what political correctness seeks to achieve today.

First of all, Jesus' self-pronunciations of being God flies in the face of political correctness, which leaves no room for God. Christ's agenda was to do the will of the Father and to show that the greatest example of power was not to control, but to wash feet (John 13:12–17). Contemporary PC culture seeks to mandate its worldview that's ultimately about power and control, while Jesus' identity was in the cross, which is all about humility, obedience, and death to self-will.

Christ's agenda was to do the will of the Father
and to show that the greatest example of
power was not to control, but to wash feet.

So how does PC thinking seek to achieve power? And what does Jesus have to say about real power to the people?

One of the mantras of political correctness is that everyone has a "right" to be right, and disavows truth beyond our experience. Jesus said that Truth is not beyond us; it was in plain view for all to see—Himself.

The problem with that comment in the PC context is that truth becomes singular and grounded in an individual—Jesus. Jesus came along to say that there is a plumb line for truth, which by design and definition does not allow deviancy from that line.

That thinking directly contradicts the current PC moral position of truth being fluid to fit the whims of each person. Kind of like "your truth is as right for you as my truth is for me." Really, I wish people would stop and think a moment before they say things like that. Or at least use another word other than *truth*.

What I do may be my desire to do it, and my right to do it, but it may not be "true" at all. It may be entirely false. However, today's PC culture has conditioned people to actually believe this nonsense. People believing whatever they want and thinking it's true has led to the mistaken notion that it's now their "right" to everything. So we have gone from believing anything is true, as long as we believe it, to "personifying" these truths with "rights."

> We have gone from believing anything is true,
> as long as we believe it, to "personifying"
> these truths with "rights."

And, yes, political correctness has a lot to say about rights. Everyone wants rights without necessarily understanding the responsibilities that come with those rights.

And here's the ultimate problem in all this. If truth is merely experiential and in our power to define it, then it serves us. We are the masters of the universe. That fits nicely into the PC mind-set of man being the ultimate god, the captains of our ships. We are in control. We have the power to decide right and wrong. And when you have that, you can create truth. Now that's appealing because it's ultimately about serving myself. Meeting my needs. And the more we serve ourselves, the more we believe that we deserve more.

And that's where the conflict comes in with what Jesus taught. Jesus sacrificed Himself for us because we did *not* deserve it; not because we deserved it, which is what political correctness would say. When a culture and its populace become more self-obsessed, they will do a lot to keep that train rolling.

Ultimately, it's just a question of power again. When Jesus challenged the politically correct groups of his day, they felt their power and control in jeopardy. It's still the same today. If there's truth beyond us, we have to answer to it. Jesus claimed to be that truth. And people did not want to answer to Him then, and they don't want to answer to Him today.

> The more we serve ourselves, the more we
> believe that we deserve more.

Unfortunately, our current generation is being raised to believe that there is no moral plumb line (absolute truth), so we do whatever we "feel" is right based on any number of influences we allow into our lives to mold and shape those beliefs. PC thinking opens the floodgates of the dam because of the belief that there are no boundaries. Problem is, if anything goes, you'll get drowned in the aftermath.

That's what we are experiencing today. We are being drowned in the flood of moral decay, and I'm not talking about sex, drugs, or rock 'n' roll. I'm talking about the decay that comes as a result of deciding there's no longer "true" truth. And when that happens, the crumbling begins. We see it first in our families, and then in how we treat each other. Next it moves to corporate ethics. That's why social problems such as hate crimes and white-collar crimes increase in a more politically correct climate.

Simply, PC thinking undermines the foundation of a culture because it removes models of selflessness as an attainable and noble goal. What does it replace them with? Models of selfishness, however subtle and cloaked they are in the delightful finery of defining one's own truth.

PC thinking undermines the foundation of a culture because it removes models of selflessness as an attainable and noble goal.

Jesus stepped into this counterfeit environment, though, to address real power to the people. He spoke about losing your life on behalf of others in order to save it. He talked about selling what we have, giving to the poor, and then following Him.

Yes, following Jesus will cost you. It will cost you your ego, your desire for self interest, your way of life.

But it will give you so much more in return.

So, what kind of power are you looking for? Be careful that you don't create a monster that turns on you.

Once we embrace Jesus,
we can begin to grasp what is true.
Truth, then, comes through a relationship,
and not through a religion, a political
movement, or accumulated knowledge.

20

Independence Day

"The truth will set you free" is a phrase often used liberally outside its original context in John 8:32. We've all heard it applied to many different situations, sometimes flippantly—from T-shirts to proclaim our independence from anything (you name it) to the inscription on the front of the Supreme Court building.

But when Jesus said those words, He was talking to people who claimed to hear from God, yet their actions spoke louder than their words. Jesus didn't mince words. He called them on the carpet. He said that if they believed Him, they would be His disciples and recognize the truth, which was that He came from God.

And if they recognized that, they'd be set free from their unbelief and all that entailed—bondage to a set of religious rules and spiritual hubris that prevented them from knowing and following God.

Further along in the Gospel of John, Jesus continues to speak of truth in His dealings with people leading to His watershed quote that pointed to Himself as *the truth*, as well as the way and the life (John 14:6). Now that *really* infuriated people.

It still does.

This statement of one way to truth conflicts with political correctness, which foists upon us a common language for postmodern thinking that encourages the notion that all truth is defined by man subjectively, rather than being defined outside of man, who is then subject to that truth. Since we don't like being anyone's subjects (that smacks of kings and despots), we rebel to think we are bound by anything. After all, independence is core to America's national identity.

Political correctness likes the road to truth to be wide, very wide, with many roads to it so that anyone can build their own road. The obvious end result is the dissolution of absolutes. But Jesus said He was *the truth.* Absolutely.

Political correctness, when confronted logically, is confusing and intellectually dishonest in its attempt to relegate truth to the wide road. Truth, by definition, must be narrow and not wide. It only allows for one way.

Most Christ-followers stand worlds apart from contemporary culture's postmodern thinking, which denies the existence of absolutes. Whereas, this is the starting point for truly understanding how the Christ-follower thinks and why he reacts to issues in the way he does.

Truth, by definition, must be narrow and
not wide. It only allows for one way.

What Jesus said to the religious people 2,000 years ago, He still says to us today: Being His disciple will allow us to know what is true. And freedom will come from that.

To the evangelical, truth is not relative. Truth is absolute and resident in a personal God, embodied in the person of Jesus Christ, who said about Himself, "I am the way and the truth and the life" (John 14:6).

So, what is the "freedom" that Jesus alludes to that knowing Him will provide?

To the Christ-follower, God created earth and man for a distinct purpose: to exhibit His creation and glory. He has set in motion principles for the maximum efficiency and co-existence of His creation to ultimately reflect that glory.

Knowing your purpose in life is the ultimate freedom. Our headlines are replete with the crazy acts of people who struggle with their purpose in life. Purpose answers the age-old questions of "Why am I here?" and, "Why do I matter?"

Knowing your purpose in life
is the ultimate freedom.

If the answer is, "You don't matter," then you act that out in many ways.

You might decide that other people don't matter, either. And if other people don't matter, and you don't matter, then you can come to the conclusion that you can walk into a school or restaurant or theater and randomly take lives. Society then looks for a "reason" for such random violence and can only point to mental illness or the availability of guns. The real answer is much deeper than that, but our PC culture refuses to address those issues because they do not fit into the box we've built to contain absolute truth.

Or you might reason that since there's no absolute standard for right or wrong, then a Bernie Maddoff or anyone else can create intricate models of deception to rob people of their life savings and ruin their lives.

I think you get the picture. The freedom Jesus talks about enables us to be free from the lies foisted upon us by a PC culture absent of absolute truth.

Here's what I mean. Science has "first principles"—universal axioms of unwavering truths woven into the very fabric of the universe, such as two times two always equals four and the physical laws of cause and effect. Likewise, there are spiritual laws of "first principles" that govern the spiritual universe. Evangelicals adhere to the biblical first principle of the fallen nature of man, which simply states that man sins because he's a sinner by nature, and not that he becomes a sinner when he sins. Man is predisposed to sin. King David rightly understood this concept when he stated, "Surely I was sinful at birth, sinful from the time my mother conceived me" (Psalm 51:5).

Because of that spiritual "first principle," which underscores the fallen nature of man and the need for redemption through Jesus Christ, the following points are keys to understanding how faith dominates the evangelical mind-set:

- Faith is the predominate grid through which Christ-followers filter most, if not all, of their lifestyle choices and around which they develop life principles.

- Issues must be deconstructed in a "faith" language and mind-set that gets past certain mental safeguards erected by evangelicals to communicate.

- There are a number of key spokespeople to utilize (or avoid) and methods of communication that are vital to understand and employ to approach evangelicals on key issues.

Ultimately, the Christ-follower's faith-based system is punctuated by the notion of faith in an object worthy of that faith, not simply faith in faith itself. That object, of course, is in a historically rooted and archaeologically tested Scripture and in the person of Jesus.

The Great Architect provided a blueprint (the Bible) by which man can know God and therefore know how to fulfill that destiny.

It is therefore the absolute authority on things spiritual and temporal to the Christ-follower.

You and I have a destiny. We can explore what that is, through God's Word and a relationship with Jesus, or allow that exploration to be blunted by the restrictiveness of PC thinking that refuses to admit to absolute truth.

You and I have a destiny. The Great Architect provided a blueprint (the Bible) by which man can know God and therefore know how to fulfill that destiny.

Jesus says that His truth is God's playbook on life, and *vital* for you and me to receive ultimate satisfaction and redemption while on earth. Political correctness calls His truth restrictive. Jesus calls it integral to true freedom: "It is for freedom that Christ has set us free. Stand firm, then, and do not let yourselves be burdened again by a yoke of slavery" (Galatians 5:1).

Once we embrace Jesus, we can begin to grasp what is true. Truth, then, comes through a relationship, and not through a religion, a political movement, or accumulated knowledge.

Jesus asks us to stay true to the One who called Himself truth incarnate. In doing so, we must communicate truth in such a way that people will not want to avoid it because we are such bad examples. Absolute truth must be handled wisely, and with humility.

Unfortunately, many in our world have not seen the wise and humble handling of this truth. It's been used many times to denounce and destroy, not affirm or heal.

It may not be politically correct to suggest there are absolutes everyone must bow to at some point. But knowing how to handle the truth Jesus was talking about will free us to be what we were created for. Each of us can know that we matter, and find the fulfillment that comes from that understanding of ourselves.

"You will know the truth, and the truth will set you free." How free do you want to be today?

Jesus asks of you the same thing He asked of people when He walked the earth.

But there is a price to be paid. And that price is what it will cost you and me to stand outside the PC thinking of our day to embrace the limitations of all truth being equal.

We must communicate truth in such a way
that people will not want to avoid it because
we are such bad examples.

The more I know Jesus, the more free I feel from the things that would enslave me to whatever my culture may impose on me to feel unloved, of no significance, or merely a pawn in some cosmic accident.

You and I matter. We have purpose and significance. Politically correct thinking and our culture would have us walk down any road we choose with no signposts and hope that we find ourselves. Jesus says there is one road. Since it's straight, you can't get lost.

I think I'd prefer to walk down one road with someone who is willing to die for me than having the choice of many roads on which to travel with those who would use me as pawns in their schemes for self-aggrandizement.

So what will you choose?

I choose real freedom—interdependence *on* Jesus rather than independence *from* Him.

"In Christ Alone"

By Keith Getty & Stuart Townend

In Christ alone my hope is found;
He is my light, my strength, my song;
This cornerstone, this solid ground,
Firm through the fiercest drought and storm.

What heights of love, what depths of peace,
When fears are stilled, when strivings cease!
My comforter, my all in all—
Here in the love of Christ I stand.

In Christ alone, Who took on flesh,
Fullness of God in helpless babe!
This gift of love and righteousness,
Scorned by the ones He came to save.

Till on that cross as Jesus died,
The wrath of God was satisfied;
For ev'ry sin on Him was laid—
Here in the death of Christ I live.

There in the ground His body lay,
Light of the world by darkness slain;
Then bursting forth in glorious day,
Up from the grave He rose again!

And as He stands in victory,
Sin's curse has lost its grip on me;
For I am His and He is mine—
Bought with the precious blood of Christ.

No guilt in life, no fear in death—
This is the pow'r of Christ in me;
From life's first cry to final breath,
Jesus commands my destiny.

No pow'r of hell, no scheme of man,
Can ever pluck me from His hand;
Till He returns or calls me home—
Here in the pow'r of Christ I'll stand.[4]

We need to get closer to Jesus,
not have the second coming
get closer to us.

21

The Psyche of the Second Coming

From time to time, there are people who like to predict the end of the world. It's nothing new. From Nostradamus to Harold Camping, there have been those who comment on these events and stir us up.

In recent memory, thanks to Mr. Camping, headlines mockingly reacted to his predictions of the world's demise that he targeted for October 21, 2012. His announcement of Armageddon provided great fodder for late-night television jokes. Possibly some interesting water-cooler talk, as well.

Political correctness really does not have much to say about when the world is going to end. There is no PC position on Armageddon that I'm aware of at the moment.

But, sometimes, our response to even the most ludicrous of statements provides insight into our culture's psyche. The preoccupation with Mr. Camping's predictions may have been an indicator of something deeper in our corporate cultural soul. Something that has to do with the larger question of our purpose on this earth.

From time to time, when our world gets a little off center

(maybe a lot off center), we worry about losing the things that make us feel safe, comfortable, untouchable. One thing about American lifestyles—we don't want anything to upset that applecart of safe and comfortable.

When our world gets a little off center,
we worry about losing the things that make
us feel safe, comfortable, untouchable.

So, every now and then when world events take a strange twist, and someone like Mr. Camping decides unilaterally to put an end date on what makes us secure, we look for signs of impending doom. There's drama enough for everyone. Wall Street failures, government gridlock, entire countries going bankrupt, unemployment, natural disasters, the political drama in the Middle East, wars and rumor of wars. Maybe Harold Camping was right about one thing. The world, as we know it, is imploding.

Can Armageddon be far behind? Will Jesus return this year? Or next?

Certainly, there may be signs that the second coming is around the corner. But who knows the length of God's block? We get so preoccupied with the idea of the second coming that it overshadows the reason for the first coming—to redeem the world, not end it.

Some people see the second coming like a script from some old Western movie, where the cavalry arrives in the nick of time, bugles blaring and rifles firing to save us from the enemy. I can see it now…Jesus riding at the head of an angelic column to "save" those who've rallied their wagons in a circle to ward off the politically correct hordes. (I had to put that in somewhere).

We want Jesus to come soon so we can go from hell on earth to heaven with Him. Isn't that a great reason for the second coming? To be relieved of our problems and pressures of living in the world?

Sure, things can be hard. But Jesus didn't tell us to wait for the second coming in order to be rid of the problems that plague us. Instead, he said, "In this world you will have trouble. But take heart! I have overcome the world" (John 16:33).

> There may be signs that the second coming
> is around the corner. But who knows
> the length of God's block?

These are comforting words when the headlines scream at us every day of things we should fear. Terrorism. Random shootings in our public schools and houses of worship. A government that seems unable to manage itself, yet alone a country.

But what's most scary is a runaway culture of self-actualization, and introspection. When it's all about me, it's never about anyone else.

And the closer we look inside, the more fear we experience. That's the problem. Jesus knew the world would try to rob us of the tranquility God wants to give us. And He pointed to Himself as the entity that could overcome anything and everything the world can throw at us so we would not have to be afraid.

That's quite a statement when you think about it. Jesus points to Himself as being the answer to our sum of all fears. He did not point to religion, or our spouses, friends, or families. And certainly not the government. He pointed to Himself.

So, if you take His Word literally, the more of Jesus, the more peace. The less of Jesus, the more fear. Notice I said *more fear* and not *less peace*.

> The more of Jesus, the more peace.
> The less of Jesus, the more fear.

You see, fear is the absence of control. People try to allay their fears by trying to exercise control over others. It happens in the boardroom, the bedroom, the classroom, and the playground. One thing that mitigates fear is having an identity and purpose to life that's grounded in Jesus and listening carefully to what He said. Read carefully the Sermon on the Mount (Matthew chapters 7–9) sometime and see if you can apply all those teachings to your everyday life. Jesus' words are so countercultural in a counterfeit world, where we're bombarded daily with completely opposite messages.

But Jesus promises to give us that identity and purpose—and the end result is a calm heart. If you place your trust in this out-of-control world's recipes for peace and success, you will also become caught up in that lack of control. And lack of control is the breeding ground of fear.

Jesus knew we did not have the power to control our lives and our destinies. It's out of our hands. We are reminded of that every time we listen to the latest news. Randomness happens.

The more randomness that scares us, the more fear. The more fear, the more anxiety and anger. Take a look at the immigration issue. We fear all the illegal aliens storming into our country, so confrontation between the two groups is on the rise.

Long story short—we need to get closer to Jesus, not have the second coming get closer to us. Wall Street can collapse. The Middle East can explode. Earthquakes can happen. But Christ promises that He is with me regardless of my situation, and that brings real comfort.

We need to get closer to Jesus,
not have the second coming get closer to us.

That's why Jesus said to occupy until He returned. And He didn't mean Wall Street. He meant to be about His business of being His hands and feet to those in need, and to tell people about the good news. Current-day saints do not forfeit the present because they are so focused on the future.

Let's use the second coming as a calling to build the kingdom of God, regardless of the work involved or forces we encounter. We already have victory over that stuff. The first coming took care of that.

I don't want to be standing
at the pearly gates someday
being politically correct,
but eternally wrong.

22

The Poker
Gospel

I have been fascinated somewhat by the amazing growth of poker competition on television. It has morphed from backroom, smoke-filled, cheesy-looking environs populated by questionable characters into luxurious casino-type surroundings attracting major movie stars dressed to the nines playing for charity on major cable networks.

Now that's transformation!

But with all the stellar changes, one thing doesn't change. The nature of the game. It's still poker. Someone wins. Most everyone else loses. Nothing is guaranteed except insecurity.

Some play for the rush. Some play for the sport. Some for money. In the end, it's all still a game. A gamble.

Now, I don't think there's anything inherently wrong...or right...about playing poker or gambling. It's just that I have such a hard time letting go of my hard-earned money for what I need to spend it on that parting with it when I don't have to leaves me kind of cold. Maybe I'm just cheap. Don't know.

Aside from my college days when a bunch of us in our dorm

would play gin rummy or poker with penny ante stakes, I only gambled one other time in my life. A bunch of us went to the track at the Meadowlands in Secaucus, New Jersey, one night and bet on the horses.

I didn't know much about horses other than watching Mr. Ed or Fury on television when I was a kid. And that I had this picture of me when I was about five sitting on a pony looking like a midget Roy Rogers on Trigger. Seems like every kid who grew up in the fifties had these quasi-cowboy shots on a pony. Must have been big business back then.

Anyway, my more knowledgeable friends helped me through the night, and I won a couple races, but lost more than I won. Overall, I came out two dollars in the red that night. It was at least a cheaper night out than going bowling, or something like that.

But one night, as I was watching a poker game on television, I mused, *All of us gamble with something in our lives.* For some of us, it's our money. For some, it's a relationship. For others, it's our bodies when we smoke, or do drugs. With most of us, though, it's with our eternal destiny.

And that's when it hit me hard.

All of us gamble with something in our lives.

Our PC world would have us believe that we can gamble with the most important aspect of our lives—our spiritual future—and always win. Political correctness believes that everybody's rules are okay, and that everyone has a winning hand in that respect. We can roll the dice, and they will always "come up seven, goin' to heaven."

Or we hope. That would be nice to believe.

But that thinking conflicts with Jesus' teachings that say the way to salvation is down the narrow road, not the wide one.

That's why the gospel is the good news—that Jesus meets us in the middle of the poker game and says that our lives needn't be a crap shoot.

And rightly so.

Because if you are to ask people why they should be allowed into heaven, or how does one get to heaven, the answer is usually that one has to be "good" or do "good" works or be a "good" person.

> Jesus meets us in the middle
> of the poker game and says that our
> lives needn't be a crap shoot.

I'm sure happy that getting into heaven is not about being good. I mean, who is going to measure how good you have to be to be good enough? Who's in charge of that deal? That scares me. As I said, I'm not a betting man, and that sounds like something out of the world series of poker on those television channels.

When playing poker and placing their bet, someone will think they have a "good" hand. Unfortunately, it's not "as good" as the next guy with the winning hand.

I want a winning hand when it comes to heaven. I want certainty. I don't want to just *think* I'm good enough, only to find out one day that all my good works and everything I did was not good enough.

Uncertainty leaves me a bit fearful. Certainty is a sign of real love. Now, that sounds more like a loving God.

And that's just one of the many reasons that the gospel is good news. And why Jesus stated with certainty throughout the Gospels that He was the way, the door, the truth, the One who assures someone of getting into heaven.

When talking about getting into heaven, the *really* good news is that Jesus replaces the word *good* with the word *grace*. *Grace* is unmerited favor, which means we did nothing to get into the game and a seat at the table. And, when the cards are dealt, we are given the winning hand. All the time. That's grace. I like that.

Jesus knew that people would like to set up their own standards and think all they had to do was live up to being "good." That's why He had to constantly remind people that their "goodness" could never match the kind of goodness required by His Father for entrance into heaven. The Old Testament is a bit stronger, and earthier, about describing men's "goodness." It says our righteousness is like a filthy menstrual rag (see Isaiah 64:6). Ouch! That hurts.

I want a winning hand when it comes to heaven. I want certainty.

Quite frankly, I'd rather not gamble on eternity. If there's one thing in this world I want to be sure of, that's it!

Can there be greater news than that?

I don't want to be standing at the pearly gates someday being politically correct, but eternally wrong.

How about you?

No eye has seen, no ear has heard, no mind has conceived what God has prepared for those who love him.

—1 Corinthians 2:9

Our citizenship is in heaven. And we eagerly await a Savior from there, the Lord Jesus Christ, who, by the power that enables him to bring everything under his control, will transform our lowly bodies so that they will be like his glorious body.

—Philippians 3:20–21

Unfortunately,
political correctness would rather
throw water on the burning bush
than fan the flame.

23

The Burning Question of the Burning Bush

One of the most intriguing encounters in all of human history is recorded in the book of Exodus. It's between Moses…and a bush. Man comes face to face with God. Well, sort of.

We're all familiar with that famous scene in *The Ten Commandments* movie with Charlton Heston as Moses, talking to the burning bush. And the bush talking back. That's a great story!

But the greater story is how it illustrates one of the Bible's most basic teachings—that God is personal, knowable, and involved. Moses found that out, for sure. When he went up to the mountain, he was a shepherd. When he came down, he was a leader. No need for graduate school. No leadership seminars. No "Pomp and Circumstance" playing in the background.

There's another interesting note to this encounter in Exodus, chapter three. The Bible says that when Moses came down the mountain, he was carrying the "staff of God." When he went up the mountain, he was just carrying a regular shepherd's staff.

God not only transformed Moses; He also transformed what Moses used for his work. The principle being that God wants us to surrender what we do, as well as who we are, in order for Him to use us.

Fast forward a thousand years or so to the time of Jesus. Jesus said that He was there at the burning bush moment: "If you believed Moses, you would believe me, for he wrote about me" (John 5:46).

> God wants us to surrender
> what we do, as well as who we are,
> in order for Him to use us.

Jesus said that He was around even before Moses and the burning bush. "I tell you the truth," Jesus declared, "before Abraham was born, I am!" (John 8:58). That comment, and a few other ones Jesus would make, often got the PC crowd of His day *really* upset. By saying what He did in the context of how he said it, Jesus was basically saying that He and God were one and the same.

Not *a* God. Not *kind of like* God. No, it was clear to the people He claimed *to be* God. That would make what He said pretty important. So important, in fact, that His words left no room for misinterpretation. Even though He often spoke in parables, Jesus was clear on that one thing. Now *that* was radical.

And just as radical was another one of His comments. He told His disciples that *they* could be burning bushes themselves! That God could now speak *through* them to others. Like Moses on that mountaintop, God wanted to transform this ragamuffin bunch of men into leaders for His kingdom. But, like Moses, they would have to do it a certain way.

Skip ahead another 2,000 years. Jesus, through His words in the Bible, tells us today that God can now speak through *you*, just as He spoke through the burning bush to Moses and to His disciples. Same God. Same opportunity. Different time.

That's right. You who are reading this book right now can also

be a burning bush. But you have to burn a certain w
Otherwise, instead of being a burning bush, you would more ..
look like a whitewashed tomb—pretty on the outside, but very
empty and hollow on the inside. That's how He described some of
the Pharisees, the PC crowd of His day. Needless to say, that did not
endear Him to those people.

Unfortunately, political correctness would rather throw water
on the burning bush than fan the flame. Political correctness wants
a level playing field for everyone. All the mountaintop experiences
must now be the same. Any road you want to take to get to your
own burning bush is okay. Any God you want to create comes with
its own burning bush. Money-back guarantee.

**You who are reading this book
right now can also be a burning bush.**

Our PC climate allows us to co-opt God simply by claiming
that there are many roads to the burning bush. But Jesus said that
God is not a commodity to be used at will by those who simply
claim to know Him. There is only one road to the burning bush,
and Jesus claimed to be it.

Just like Moses and the disciples before us, Jesus calls us to
surrender who we are and what we do so God can reshape it all
to accomplish His purposes. But no longer being in charge can be
scary to many. Even more because, in our PC world, we are told
to hold tight to who we are and do what "feels right" to us. Since
there are no moral absolutes, there's no need to surrender anything
about ourselves that needs changing. We prefer to hold tightly onto
the things we own, and to use them for our own purposes, rather
than God's.

The road to the burning bush, Jesus said, came with a price. "I tell
you the truth, unless a kernel of wheat falls to the ground and dies, it
remains only a single seed. But if it dies, it produces many seeds. The

man who loves his life will lose it, while the man who hates his life in this world will keep it for eternal life" (John 12:24–26).

That price cost Jesus His earthly life. It will also cost you yours.

Jesus asks us to become a "burning bush," so people can see God. If that's the mountaintop experience in life you're looking for, welcome to the fraternity of the burning bushes!

I tell you the truth, unless a kernel of wheat falls to the ground and dies, it remains only a single seed. But if it dies, it produces many seeds. The man who loves his life will lose it, while the man who hates his life in this world will keep it for eternal life.

—JOHN 12:24–26

In the economy of the kingdom
of God, no one is greater because he gives,
and no one is lesser because he receives.
The world needs to see that.

24

A Vagrant Faith

A plaque hung on the wall of the School of Public Communication at Boston University when I was there during all the student unrest of the late 1960s/early '70s. It said, "Be Ashamed to Die Until You've Achieved Some Victory for Humanity." It was attributed to the great American educator of the late nineteenth-century Horace Mann.

When I first saw it, and as a product of the '60s, I was a bit cynical of things that sounded so lofty as that quote. By the time I graduated four years later, and had come to faith in Christ, I had a different perception of that quote. Jesus could have said it.

The interesting thing about being a Christ-follower is that Jesus expects you to actually believe everything He said and be His representative here on earth. He told His followers, "Anyone who has faith in me will do what I have been doing. He will do even greater things than these" (John 14:12).

You ask, "How could anyone do greater things than Jesus?"

Notice He didn't say that we would do the same works. No, He said greater works. What could be greater than raising the dead, feeding 5,000 people with five fish and a few loaves of bread, and healing someone born blind or paralyzed or deaf?

And then it dawned on me that Jesus was really speaking to his followers who would come after Him. They would speak to millions, change the course of history, devote themselves to starting schools, orphanages, hospitals, leper colonies, and silently and prayerfully take down corrupt governments and institutions that enslaved people. These *are* greater works.

But an even more relevant concept in that statement is one about identity. Jesus was telling His followers that they would have a new identity. They would be known by one glaring characteristic—their love for one another. It was their oneness that would set them apart from everyone else. And it would include people of every race, nationality, male and female, young and old. You name it. Never before was there such a radical statement of forming a new ethnicity of people of every color and race. These would be called Christ-followers.

Jesus was saying that one of the unique traits of His followers would be that God favors diversity above uniformity—that people would be different yet one, and not all the same and one.

> Never before was there such a radical
> statement of forming a new ethnicity
> of people of every color and race.
> These would be called Christ-followers.

That thought was driven home to me in one of those rare incidents when you really believe God is speaking to you—not audibly, but in that still, small voice that rings loudly in your heart and soul that some observation or truth was just revealed to you.

In 1991, Billy Graham held a crusade for the North Jersey/New York City metro area. I was involved as a vice-chair of the North Jersey Crusade and Publicity Chair. As with most of Dr. Graham's crusades, his team comes in about a year prior to the actual crusade and begins to set up the logistics for pulling off a massive event. A number of individuals with a variety of skill sets are recruited as volunteers, and pastors and clergy of all denominations and races become part of the steering committee.

At one of our committee meetings, a number of us were gathered in one room. I looked around to a group represented by every strain of African-American, Caucasian, Asian, and Hispanic leaders. As each person stood to introduce themselves to the group, I heard that still, small voice say these words: "In this I am well pleased." I understood this to be from God's Spirit, confirming that we know our identity best when it's part of the larger body of Christ. When we lose ourselves in the mixture, we're stronger.

You see, we are made to be interdependent, not independent or dependent. John Donne wrote, "No man is an island," and he was right.[5] The genius of America is that we are different, yet one, not that we are all the same and one. And America is great because it reflects the biblical principle of true diversity—*e pluribus unum*.

We know our identity best when
it's part of the larger body of Christ.
We are made to be interdependent,
not independent or dependent.

In this context, let me suggest that we best identify as a Christ-follower to the world around us when we appear as vagrants. There's an old line that a Christian may use to identify heaven as the ultimate destination: "This (earth) is not my home; I'm just passing through."

How many times have you heard someone say that? How many times have you said that? Sometimes we casually (and maybe a little too snobbishly) use that phrase to communicate our reluctance to identify with the "world" or "worldly practices" in order to stand apart and in contrast to what's going on in culture all around us.

The problem with standing apart from someone is that you never have a chance to stand with them.

The other side of that coin is that some of us feel that we have to "relate" to our culture, as that's what Jesus did. So we try to retrofit Jesus to fit our culture, and wind up losing the whole purpose of our faith, which is to represent Christ to the culture.

> The problem with standing apart
> from someone is that you never have
> a chance to stand with them.

Representing Christ will often take us in opposite directions of our culture. But that does not mean separation from people. To the contrary, the opposite direction is not about geography, but about bringing a lifestyle and a love that is separate.

One of the great things about what Christ offers everyone is a new economy to define His vagrant faith. In His economy of the kingdom of God, no one is greater because he gives, and no one is lesser because he receives. The world needs to see that.

They need to see the vagrancy of our faith, which is to give everything, yet own nothing. The vagrant faith understands that poverty and ownership are part of the same lifestyle. In Christ, I have everything I need, yet own nothing. Jesus pointed out how much His Father cares for things seemingly less significant than people (Matthew 6:28–30), so does it not make sense that He would care for us even more?

> In His economy of the kingdom of God,
> no one is greater because he gives,
> and no one is lesser because he receives.
> The world needs to see that.

Yet, in the same breath, Jesus likens His disciples to Himself, as people having no place to rest their heads (Matthew 8:20). Jesus is saying that we have everything we need in the context of having nothing!

The apostle Paul said that he had learned to be content in any condition in which he found himself because he understood that his wealth was in his relationship to Christ, not in his possessions or position.

The apostle Paul said that he had learned to be content in any condition in which he found himself because he understood that his wealth was in his relationship to Christ, not in his possessions or position.

In contrast, the American perspective is to acquire wealth, or at least comfort. The focus on acquiring all of this is illusory, says Jesus. And it's one reason America is in sad shape today. We do not regard ourselves as vagrants, but as property owners. Jesus confronts us as he did the rich young ruler and told him to go sell all he owned, and then come follow Him. Scripture says this was a hard saying, and the young man went away sad (Matthew 19:16–22).

Jesus confronts each of us, as well, to ask a similar question: "What in your life are you holding on to that would come before Me?" Jesus is talking so far beyond economics, rich or poor. Having little money or much money is not what makes one rich or poor. Rather, Jesus is saying that one's richness is the degree to which one wants to conform to Him, and to understand that all they have is not theirs, but God's.

Simply, Jesus' definition of poverty was not about one's material or economic condition, but about one's mind-set. Anything we value more than obedience to Him is a distraction—be it material, emotional, relational—and supplants our faith in Christ with a made-up faith to conform to our own image.

The incarnation of Christ was not just to save people from themselves, but to show them a walking, breathing, working model of God's kingdom. Jesus understood that man's satisfaction with himself and his world is best understood in terms of the spiritual part of man. Poverty of the spirit is what really keeps people enslaved. Being poor materially may keep one less comfortable, but not necessarily less joyful or content.

The incarnation of Christ was not
just to save people from themselves,
but to show them a walking, breathing,
working model of God's kingdom.

Being rich spiritually gives us joy, inner peace, and the security that everyone strives for, yet cannot achieve with material possessions. Jesus wanted to communicate a spiritual understanding of our relationship to this world. When we recognize that, we have true wealth.

So, may the vagrant faith spirit of having everything, and owning nothing, be your lifestyle. When you find that, you find your true identity in Christ. And you can go out and change the world... and do the greater works that Jesus was talking about.

Now, that's something I can buy into. And I can buy it at no charge. Such a deal.

Endnotes

1 Excerpt from *The God Who Is There,* by Francis A. Schaeffer, 30th Anniversary Edition (Westmont, IL: InterVarsity Press, 1998).

2 "ACLU complains about religious concert," by Heather Hollingsworth, in Times-Herald.com, Newman, Georgia, published Saturday, December 24, 2011, http://www.times-herald.com/printerFriendly/ACLU -complains-about-religious-concert-in-Missouri, accessed August 26, 2014.

3 Copyright: © 2008 TwoNords Music (ASCAP), (all rights administered worldwide by Music Services, Inc., www.musicservices.org) and Integrity's Praise! Music (BMI) (admin at emicmgpublishing.com). All rights reserved. Used by permission.

4 Copyright © 2002 Thankyou Music (PRS) (adm. worldwide at CapitolCMGPublishing.com excluding Europe which is adm. by Integritymusic.com). All rights reserved. Used by permission.

5 "No Man Is an Island," in *Meditation XVII,* John Donne (1572-1631). The Literature Network, http://www.online-literature.com/donne/409/, accessed 8/23/2014.

Acknowledgments

It would be hard to be who I am today without the influence of some great people in my life through the years. To Dr. Doug Culver and Bill Iverson for teaching me early on the discipline of thinking through my faith and owning it; to all my friends in the fraternities of Christian radio and Christian music who have supported me in my work of 40 years; to my dear friends Don Osgood and Dave Swanson, who are no longer with us but were there for a young man as patient, gracious mentors of how to live a godly life; to my Renaissance Communications family (Wendy, Joe, Tricia, Lyn) who stood with me through the years and who provided a great sounding board for all my ramblings; and to my church family at PBC and home group (Frank, Robyn, Mike, Siegfried, and Lyn) that act as my decompression chambers that allows me to be who I am.

Each of us is the aggregate of all those who have crossed our paths in our lives. I have been fortunate to have had the best of all worlds. And finally to my publisher, Carlton Garborg, and an amazing editor in Ramona Tucker, for believing in me and this message. I am deeply grateful for your help in bringing this dream to fruition!

About the Author

JOE BATTAGLIA is the founder and president of Renaissance Communications, a company specializing in providing media platforms for organizations and gifted communicators of the faith and values message, whose clients include Dr. Steve Brown and the Key Life Radio Network, Affirm Films/Sony Pictures Entertainment, Provident Films, actress Shari Rigby, author/pastor Tullian Tchividjian, Pure Flix Entertainment, and Feed The Children.

Joe is also an executive producer of the nationally syndicated radio program "Keep the Faith," heard nationally in over 200 markets and numerous countries overseas.

Renaissance has been heavily involved in the promotion of successful hit movies to the faith-based marketplace, such as *The Passion, The Lion, The Witch & The Wardrobe, The Polar Express, Facing the Giants, Fireproof, Courageous, Soul Surfer, Son of God, God's Not Dead, Heaven Is For Real, The Giver, When the Game Stands Tall,* and *Left Behind.*

Highly active in the Christian music industry, Joe served on the board of Gospel Music Association (GMA) for 19 years, was chairman of the National Christian Radio Association (NCRS) for 14 years, and currently sits on the boards of the Walter Hoving Home in Garrison, New York, and the WAY-FM Radio Network.

Prior to forming Renaissance in 1992, Joe was VP of

Communicom Corp. of America, the then parent company of WWDJ/New York, WZZD/Philadelphia, and KSLR/San Antonio. He was with Communicom for over 18 years, eight as General Manager of the flagship station WWDJ from 1982–1990.

From 1979–1995, he also was a partner in Living Communications, parent company of WLIX, Long Island, NY and WLVX, Hartford, CT.

In 1991, Joe penned his first book, *A New Suit for Lazarus* (Thomas Nelson).

He attended Boston University, graduating magna cum laude with a BS in Journalism.

Joe can still be found at times hanging around some street corners in North Jersey with old friends singing doo-wop songs, because that's where Jesus might be if He were around today.

www.ThePoliticallyIncorrectJesus.com

Notes

Notes

Notes

Notes

Notes

www.ThePoliticallyIncorrectJesus.com